"If you long for a relationship with God that is deeper, richer, and more intimate than you've ever known before, read this book. In *Experiencing God's Presence*, Linda Evans Shepherd reveals the secrets of learning how to listen to God during your prayer times. Each chapter is filled with practical, biblical tools that will enrich your prayer life and draw you closer to the heart of the Father."

Carol Kent, speaker and author,
When I Lay My Isaac Down

Praise for *When You Don't Know What to Pray*

"Linda has used powerful prayer to overcome the worst of circumstances, and you can too. She does not share pat answers, she shares truth that will transform your life. Are you ready to learn her prayer secrets? Bow your head and pray your way through this book."

LeAnn Thieman, coauthor, *Chicken Soup for the Christian Woman's Soul and Chicken Soup for the Christian Soul 2*

"Linda uses both breathtaking and tender experiences to move us through the pages of this inspiring and humorous look at the power of prayer. She teaches us the keys to prayer, demonstrating through practical prayer examples how to pray, what to pray, and when to pray. You will be encouraged when you read this book."

Thelma Wells, author; speaker,
Women of Faith Conferences;
president, A Woman of God Ministries,
Dallas, Texas

"Linda Evans Shepherd is a woman of prayer, and in a world of crisis, change, and constant challenges, what woman doesn't need to learn more about the praying life? Pick up this book to gain an encouraged and equipped heart."

Pam Farrel, international speaker; relationship specialist; author, *Men Are Like Waffles, Women Are Like Spaghetti*

"The book's strength is Shepherd's heart for prayer and tenderness for her readers. Recommend to people who are struggling through difficult circumstances and to pastors and group leaders."

CBA Retailers + Resources

Experiencing God's Presence

Learning to Listen While You Pray

Linda Evans Shepherd

Revell

a division of Baker Publishing Group
Grand Rapids, Michigan

© 2013 by Linda Evans Shepherd

Published by Revell
a division of Baker Publishing Group
P.O. Box 6287, Grand Rapids, MI 49516-6287
www.revellbooks.com

Printed in the United States of America

Library of Congress Cataloging-in-Publication Data
Shepherd, Linda E., 1957–
    Experiencing God's presence : learning to listen while you pray / Linda
Evans Shepherd.
        pages cm
    Includes bibliographical references.
    ISBN 978-0-8007-2214-2 (pbk.)
    1. Prayer—Christianity. I. Title.
BV210.3.S5476 2013
248.3′2—dc23   2013013665

Some names and details have been changed to protect privacy.

Unless otherwise indicated, Scripture quotations are from the Holy Bible, New International Version®. NIV®. Copyright © 1973, 1978, 1984, 2011 by Biblica, Inc.™ Used by permission of Zondervan. All rights reserved worldwide. www.zondervan.com

Scripture quotations labeled GW are from GOD'S WORD®. © 1995 God's Word to the Nations. Used by permission of Baker Publishing Group.

Scripture quotations labeled KJV are from the King James Version of the Bible.

Scripture quotations labeled Message are from *The Message* by Eugene H. Peterson, copyright © 1993, 1994, 1995, 2000, 2001, 2002. Used by permission of NavPress Publishing Group. All rights reserved.

Scripture quotations labeled NKJV are from the New King James Version. Copyright © 1982 by Thomas Nelson, Inc. Used by permission. All rights reserved.

Scripture quotations labeled NLT are from the *Holy Bible*, New Living Translation, copyright © 1996, 2004, 2007 by Tyndale House Foundation. Used by permission of Tyndale House Publishers, Inc., Carol Stream, Illinois 60188. All rights reserved.

Scripture quotations labeled NLV are from New Life Version © Christian Literature International.

Scripture quotations labeled TLB are from *The Living Bible*, copyright © 1971. Used by permission of Tyndale House Publishers, Inc., Wheaton, Illinois 60189. All rights reserved.

13 14 15 16 17 18 19   7 6 5 4 3 2 1

In memory of my friend and faithful reader
Nancy Shizue Tsuji Whang.

Heaven is more glorious than you can imagine.

Contents

Acknowledgments   9

Introduction: Come Boldly to God   11

1. Praying to Experience God's Presence   15
2. Experience God's Transforming Power   29
3. Experience God's Blessings   45
4. Experience God's Hope   59
5. Experience Trusting in God   75
6. Experience Deliverance from Evil   89
7. Experience God's Healing Power   103
8. Experience Praising God   119
9. Experience God's Love   135
10. Experience the Joy of the Lord   151
11. Experience the Peace of God   167
12. Experience More of God   181

Discussion Questions   201
Notes   215

Acknowledgments

What a challenging year! How would I ever have gotten through it without my loving husband and children? Thank you, dear family.

Also, a special thanks to my editor, Vicki Crumpton, and my agent, Janet Kobobel Grant, as well as all my wonderful friends at Baker Publishing Group. Thank you for all you do to get the messages of my heart into the hands of readers.

And thanks be to God. If it weren't for his voice of encouragement, you would not be holding this book in your hands.

Introduction

Come Boldly to God

Let us therefore come boldly to the throne of grace, that we
may obtain mercy and find grace to help in time of need.

Hebrews 4:16 NKJV

Today, I have a vibrant relationship with God, but this was
not always the case. Though I'd had a special love for the
Lord since childhood, I felt lonely. I knew I could talk to him
in my heart, but as far as I could tell, God either couldn't
or wouldn't talk back. I'd decided God was silent, and his
silence felt deafening.

Of course, I knew God used the Bible to guide my life,
but I couldn't shake the feeling that there had to be more. I
longed for something beyond my one-sided relationship with
him, to see him, to hear him, face-to-face. But I figured that
wouldn't happen until I graduated to heaven, and I wasn't
ready for *that*. I felt stuck because my timid, little prayers
didn't seem to connect me to God on a deeper level. I wasn't
even sure how to pray correctly, effectively, or in a way that

helped me feel the warmth of God's presence. It seemed to me that my prayers were going only as high as the ceiling. That's why I set out on a quest to try to figure out how to crack the prayer code.

Then the day came when I found myself listening to a speaker who explained that I needed to create an elaborate list of requests to bring daily before the Lord. The speaker even showed a clever notebook she'd developed that would help me organize my list. "The exciting part," she explained, "is getting to put a check mark next to the requests as God answers."

> *I discovered that as I reached for a more vibrant friendship with God, he reached right back with his presence.*

I was intrigued, so I dutifully bought the notebook, made my list, and carefully read it to the Lord for an entire month. But I felt like I was merely reciting a shopping list to God. I couldn't help but shake my head and grin, for if my husband communicated with me only through a list of everything he wanted me to do, I would certainly get annoyed.

Not wanting to annoy God, I abandoned my list until a couple years later when I happened to find the notebook in the bottom of a drawer. When I opened it and read through my original requests, I was amazed that I was able to pull out my pen and put a check mark next to every petition I'd jotted down two years earlier. Despite the fact I'd been worried that my prayer list bored God, I realized God had not only heard my prayers but also graciously responded with many miraculous results, even long after I'd forgotten to pray. This exercise proved to me that I could boldly come to his throne of grace, even when I came with a long list of prayer requests.

Still, I felt God was too majestic and powerful for me to think of him only as my "heavenly bag boy," and I knew my prayer life had a ways to grow if I were to develop the vibrant, two-way relationship I longed to have with the Lord of the universe.

Today, though I still keep prayer lists, I no longer recite them daily. I do review and update them monthly, and I do so enjoy checking off his answers. However, I'm glad my prayer journey didn't get lost in my lists but continued as I pushed to connect with God.

These days, I can tell you that my prayer times bring me the closeness to God I'd longed for. I discovered that as I reached for a more vibrant friendship with God, he reached right back with his presence. Not only has he given me a deepening relationship with him, but he's also given me answered prayers, joy, and peace. Most importantly, he's given me his presence, and he allows me to hear his loving voice.

Now, through the pages of this book, I'm going to share what I learned as I show you (and perhaps your study group) how to pray and to listen to God's voice. These prayer experiences as well as discussion questions at the end of the book will change your life and draw you closer still.

1

Praying to Experience God's Presence

Draw near to God and He will draw near to you.

James 4:8 NKJV

I recently told a group, "As the times grow darker, you need to be able to hear the voice of God like never before. If God tells you to turn right, turn right. But if he tells you to turn left, turn left. Your life could depend on hearing and following God's voice."

A couple weeks later, a series of deadly tornadoes swept through that town, and though there was loss of life, not one of those who had been in my audience perished. One woman later told me, "My husband was driving when he felt a strong urge to turn right. If he had turned left, he would have found himself in the path of one of the tornadoes. He's alive today because he followed the voice of the Lord."

We must learn to hear and follow God's voice now, before it's too late.

In Matthew 25, Jesus tells a story of ten bridesmaids who were waiting along the road for a wedding procession to pass. Though each of the young women had brought a lamp to shine into the lengthening shadows, only five had brought enough oil to refill their lamps. Soon the darkness deepened and the sound of crickets lulled the women to sleep. Near midnight, the shouts of the bridegroom startled them awake. He was coming for his bride!

Your life could depend on hearing and following God's voice.

Only the women who were able to refill their lamps were ready to follow the groom. The other five ran into town to try to buy more oil and completely missed the wedding march. When they returned from their failed mission, they found the door to the wedding feast bolted shut and discovered they had been left outside to suffer the darkness. Jesus ended the parable by saying, "So stay awake and be prepared, for you do not know the date or moment of my return" (v. 13 TLB).

Though the bridesmaids heard the voice of the groom, they were not ready to follow him because they did not have enough oil to light their way. The hour is already late, and the darkness continues to deepen. If you hear the voice of the Lord, will you have enough oil to light your way so that you can follow him when he calls?

But first ask yourself, "Is my lamp even lit?"

To ignite your lamp, please pray the following:

Dear Lord,
   The only way I can draw close to you is to enter through the door named Jesus, who said, "I am the

*way and the truth and the life. No one comes to the
Father except through me" (John 14:6). Therefore,
Lord, I acknowledge Jesus, your only Son, who came
to free me from sin and death by paying for my sins on
the cross. I also acknowledge that Jesus rose from the
dead so that the power of sin and death is broken in my
life.*

*I receive Jesus's gift of grace and say, "Thank you,
Jesus, for all you've done for me. Thank you that your
grace and righteousness cover my sins so I can walk
with a holy God." In Jesus's name, amen.*

If you said the above prayer for the very first time, the
lamp of your soul has been set ablaze with the very presence
of God's Holy Spirit. Now that
the flame is lit, let's look at the
secret to keeping the flame of
the Spirit burning bright.

One of the best ways to fan
this flame is through prayer.
Pioneer missionary L. B. Cowman once wrote, "Prayer brings
us closer to God and helps us
understand his purpose for us.
It is through prayer that we par-
ticipate in a conversation with
God."[1]

> *Not only do we need
> to know how to talk
> to God, but we also
> need to learn how
> to stay in continual
> conversation
> with him.*

This is key. Not only do we need to know how to talk
to God, but we also need to learn how to stay in continual
conversation with him.

The real question is this. If God loves you enough to send
his Son to rescue you, then do you think this God is interested
in seeing you draw close enough to hear his voice?

A thousand times yes!

And that's exactly what this book is about—prayer, or conversations, to help you draw closer to God, to help you more deeply experience his love for you. Together, we will pray through this book. As we learn to hear God's voice, we will experience a closeness to God that will ignite our very beings with even more of the oil of his loving presence.

Prayer, Our Connection to God

With all the darkness descending upon our world, with all the storms sweeping across our land, and with all the heartache that complicates our lives, how is it possible to connect with this God who says he loves us?

The solution is prayer.

Will Davis, author of *Pray Big*, writes:

> Prayer brings you closer to God, and you'll need all the intimacy with God you can get when the storms break out. I'm sure this is partly why Paul encouraged us to "pray without ceasing" (1 Thess. 5:17 NASB). He knew firsthand the importance of storing up spiritual intimacy for those difficult times of suffering that would drain him dry. Paul . . . kept his intimacy with God intact throughout his trials because he was close to God *before* the trouble came. Peacetime praying helps you build the intimacy with God you'll need to weather your storms.[2]

As Davis makes clear, it's good to know God in times of peace, but it's especially good to know God in times of trouble.

Behold Jesus

Peter and the disciples were ready for trouble; after all, they were following that exciting young rabbi named Jesus. Not

18

only did he talk about the kingdom of God in a fresh way, but he also rebuked the pompous religious leaders with names like "blind guides" and "whitewashed tombs full of bones." He also favored men more like them—tax collectors and fishermen. But besides that, Jesus touched the untouchable and healed the sick. Surely, as Peter believed, Jesus had come in the power of God to free them from Roman rule. If that turned out to be the case, Peter and the disciples were ready to stand with him and fight.

> *It's good to know God in times of peace, but it's especially good to know God in times of trouble.*

But the day Jesus fed the five thousand with five loaves and two fish Peter sensed a new excitement among the people. He heard them murmur as he helped gather the leftovers, "Surely, this is the one who will save us from the Romans." Others joked, "Let us all become his disciples and he will feed us fish sticks from heaven."

Peter couldn't help but grin, for surely the time for Jesus to rise to power was upon them.

That evening, Jesus sent Peter and the others to cross the Sea of Galilee by boat, promising to join them later. As the men pushed off from shore, Peter could see the figure of Jesus as he began his solitary climb up the mountain to pray.

But Peter lost sight of Jesus as the sun slid past the horizon and a turbulent cloud settled upon the lake.

As the wind began to pick up, growing swells threatened to capsize their boat, and Peter and the disciples fought to keep it afloat. They desperately hoped they would not join the fishermen of storms past who rested in their watery graves beneath them.

About 4 a.m., a flash of lightning lit the figure of a man who seemed to glide across the churning waves with his robes billowing behind him. Peter was the first to scream, "A ghost!"

Jesus called back, "Don't be afraid! It's only me."

Peter shielded his eyes from the pelting rain. "Lord, if it is really you, tell me to come to you, walking on the water."

"All right," Jesus said, "come!"

Peter focused his eyes on the Lord and stepped onto the lake. The surface of the water held Peter's weight, and he took one step, then another. But when the wind-whipped spray splashed his face and a wave swelled beneath his feet, Peter made the mistake of looking down. In that horrible moment, Peter went under. As his arms flailed against the churning water, he managed to lift his chin above the waves and cry, "Save me, Lord!"

Jesus calmly watched as Peter thrashed at his feet before reaching down to clasp Peter's hand and pulling him to stand on the surface of the water. Jesus asked, "Where was your faith? Why did you doubt me?"

Instead of answering, Peter clung to the Master's arm, and together they walked back to the boat. When they climbed inside, the wind grew silent, and peace rested upon the lake.

Peter and the disciples were so awed that they bowed before Jesus, saying, "You really are the Son of God!" (based on Matt. 14:15–33).

I don't know about you, but I have to admire Peter for even getting out of the boat in the middle of a stormy lake. If we can learn to behold Jesus the way Peter beheld him on the Sea of Galilee, then we too can walk on top of the storms of life without having to thrash among the waves. We'll be able to walk over any of our circumstances, no matter how difficult.

However, when we take our eyes off Jesus and stare into the storm, we will find ourselves in over our heads. If this should happen to you, don't panic. Jesus will be right there, calmly, lovingly, reaching down to grasp your hand as you cry, "Save me, Lord!" His fingers will entwine with yours, and once you are holding on to his strong grip, you will be safe from any storm, no matter how ferocious.

In each chapter of this book, we will stop to behold the Lord in prayer. Beholding the Lord will help us move closer to him, and we will be able to step through any storm as if we were stepping through a mud puddle. We might get our feet wet, but there will be no chance of drowning.

I know what I'm talking about. A few weeks ago I was feeling the wrath of an unexpected storm. With both of my parents in the middle of health crises and in and out of the hospital, I found myself hopping on and off airplanes so I could rush to help. But by dropping everything, my to-do list threatened to overwhelm me. Besides caring for my parents, I was speaking at conferences and had other conferences to plan. Plus, book marketing projects had already been set in motion that required my immediate attention. Websites needed to be created, plus my nonprofit ministry was in the middle of launching a new online ministry for the suicidal that would require hours of my time. I was overwhelmed.

Beholding the Lord will help us move closer to him, and we will be able to step through any storm as if we were stepping through a mud puddle. We might get our feet wet, but there will be no chance of drowning.

Just where, I wondered, *am I going to find the time to work on my new book?*

Late one night as I lay my head on my pillow, my mind begin to spin as I thought through all I had to accomplish in the next few months. My parents were still in crisis, one of my children had hit a difficult snag, and my to-do list was growing faster than I could possibly keep up with. "Help me, Lord! Help me!" I cried from my bed as sheer panic drummed my heart.

With tears, I told the Lord, "I am only one little gal. How is it you've called me to accomplish so much in these next few weeks? How am I supposed to achieve all these things you have put on my plate plus deal with my family's crises?

Behold me, I heard him whisper.

So I tried to imagine what Peter must have seen when he saw the Lord walking across the top of the water on the Sea of Galilee. But instead of seeing the Lord, all I could see was a blizzard of paperwork falling around me, each page scrawled with yet another "to do" written in black marker.

As I watched this paper blizzard fall around me, I saw the pages of my to-do list landing then floating on the turbulent Sea of Galilee. That's when I saw him. Jesus was walking toward me, over the tops of the floating papers.

Behold me, he whispered.

As his face came into focus, I took a step toward him, my foot secure on one of the many floating papers around me. Miraculously, both the paper and the wave held my weight.

Behold me, he encouraged as I continued to look at him.

I took another step, then another as my eyes locked on Jesus's face.

When I reached him, he said, "Linda, you can only walk through this storm if you behold me."

My heart quit racing and my tears stopped falling. The

Lord himself had shown me that he would get me through my storm of to-dos but only if I kept my mind stayed on him. I was reminded of Isaiah 26:3–4, which states, "He will keep in perfect peace all those who trust in him, whose thoughts turn often to the Lord! Trust in the Lord God always, for in the Lord Jehovah is your everlasting strength" (TLB).

Now it's time to consider one of the prayers we will pray together in every chapter: the behold him prayer. These are not canned words but prayers to help you experience or behold God in a fresh way. Are you ready to pray? Just say the following words aloud or in the quietness of your heart.

Beholding Jesus in Prayer

Dear Lord,

I have been so worried about _____, even frantic. I feel like I'm in over my head, thrashing in the waves that are trying to pull me under. So now, desperate for you, I lift my chin above the swirling water and cry, "Save me, Lord!"

I trust that you are taking my hand to lift me out of the storm. I look to you and know you are lovingly saying, "Why didn't you trust me?"

I'm sorry, Lord, and now I will trust you. I will behold you as together we take the first step over the storm that once held me captive.

I am freed from being a captive of the storm as I behold you. I behold you and your love, grace, kindness, and mercy. I trust you, Jesus. I follow you. I love and adore you. I thank you for loving me so much that you put your Holy Spirit inside me so that you are forever in my heart. In Jesus's name, amen.

23

Listening Prayer

When I was a girl, I loved to search through my *Weekly Reader*, a colorful flyer that pitched books to school kids. Every Monday afternoon, I'd pore over this paper, putting a check mark next to almost every book I saw. Later, I'd have to go back and erase all but my top selections so as to stay within my small book budget.

But one day, when I was in sixth grade, my shy, bookworm self was stunned to see a title that I was sure only God himself knew I needed. It was too good to be true, for there it was, a book called *How to Talk to Boys*. I checked the box, tucked the form and my dollars in an envelope, and turned my order in to my teacher.

When my book arrived, I snuck it home in my book bag and headed to my room, where I carefully locked the door to escape the prying eyes of my little brother. There at my white princess desk I began poring over the book's pages. What I learned that afternoon changed my life because I discovered that the secret to talking to a boy had nothing to do with reciting a list of your good qualities as tidbits to bait your hook. I found out that a, "Hey, Joe, did you know I've played the piano for five years and that I like to write poems?" was simply not a good conversation starter.

Instead, this wonder-of-wonders book explained that if you wanted to successfully talk to a boy, you needed to ask him questions such as, "Hey, Joe, what's your favorite television show?" or "So, Joe, what's your favorite sport?" I learned that by getting a boy to talk about himself you could actually have a real conversation with him, which could lead to a boyfriend! Oh, happy day!

As I discovered, the technique worked well. I've now been married for over thirty years. And I have to admit, I still use these conversation-building pointers whenever I strike up a conversation with a person I'm meeting for the first time—not as a way to get a date but as a way to get to know them. But that leads me to ask, what would happen if we tried using conversation triggers with God?

Prayer is much sweeter when we realize it's an act that can be supernatural, that can tap into God's holy presence. We can ask questions, then quietly listen for his response.

But one of the best God-conversation starters I've found is Scripture. Let's try it now.

1. First, ask God to quiet your mind and to speak to you. Then read Psalm 23 (NLT):

> The LORD is my shepherd;
>> I have all that I need.
> He lets me rest in green meadows;
>> he leads me beside peaceful streams.
> He renews my strength.
> He guides me along right paths,
>> bringing honor to his name.
> Even when I walk
>> through the darkest valley,
> I will not be afraid,
>> for you are close beside me.
> Your rod and your staff
>> protect and comfort me.
> You prepare a feast for me
>> in the presence of my enemies.
> You honor me by anointing my head with oil.
>> My cup overflows with blessings.
> Surely your goodness and unfailing love will pursue
>>> me
>> all the days of my life,
> and I will live in the house of the LORD
>> forever.

2. Next, read these verses again, slowly, and write down thoughts that occur to you. Then read them again, emphasizing different words or phrases. Then write down any more thoughts that occur to you.

_____

_____

_____

_____

_____

_____

3. Read over what you have written to discern if God is speaking to you. You may hear from him right away, or you may have to continue to practice this listening prayer as you continue to meditate on his Word. When trying to hear God, keep in mind that God will never speak to you in a way that goes against or violates his Word.

Making It Personal

Below is an example of what I think God is saying. Please pray:

Dear Lord,

You want to lead and guide me. You also want me to rest in you, to sit quietly and enjoy your presence. You've come to give me refreshment, to serve me with the peace and joy of your very presence. Just as you were with Peter when you walked with him over the waves in the Sea of Galilee, you are with me. I am beholding you now, and I am not afraid. No matter where my journey leads, you will go beside me, never leaving my side.

You protect me, anoint me, and even honor me before those who don't even like me. You do this not because I deserve any sort of royal treatment but because I am so dear to you. And now out of the overflow of my heart, I thank you, for you are also very dear to me. In Jesus's name, amen.

2

Experience God's Transforming Power

Prayer transforms lives by God's grace at work in hearts.

Rick Osborn[1]

Theologian and author Stanley G. Grenz once wrote, "The greatest challenge that we face today is the challenge to pray. Meeting this challenge requires that we merely cease talking about prayer and begin to pray."[2]

I agree with Grenz, which is why we will stop to pray throughout this book. Knowing how to pray will make an incredible difference in our relationship with God and also in our lives.

Look at it this way. Imagine you're a young, single man and you've just asked the girl in your accounting class for a date because you're genuinely interested in getting to know her. The two of you agree to meet at your favorite coffee shop to chat. When you're finally sitting across from her, sipping a steaming mocha latte, you ask, "How do you think you did on the test this morning?"

She shrugs. "Fine."

Silence.

"So, tell me about your family?"

"Not much to say, really."

More silence.

"How are your classes going?"

"They're going."

It's so quiet you can hear the crickets chirping.

> *Knowing how to pray will make an incredible difference in our relationship with God and also in our lives.*

Can you imagine how you would feel if the conversation stayed on this level, especially when you knew this interesting young woman was holding back? You would have to wonder if she was bored, really didn't want to hang out with you, or perhaps was just nervous.

Regardless of the reason, if the conversations between the two of you stayed forever stalled, it would be difficult to grow a deeper friendship.

Imagine your prayer life following this example. Maybe that's not so difficult to imagine because all you ever pray is an old line like, "God, bless me and mine. Amen."

If this is you, know you're not alone in your struggle to communicate with God. But regardless, it's hard to build a deeper relationship with God when your prayer life is stuck in neutral. Sure, God still loves you, but think of all you'll miss by not becoming more invested in your relationship with him.

But what if the problem is that you really don't feel comfortable talking to God and you worry you might say the wrong thing to him.

Many people are worried about this, and I can understand the concern. I mean, God is the most awesome and powerful being in the universe. But treating God like a stranger you just met on the subway is not the answer. Perhaps what you really need are a few basic conversation starters, such as these prayer ABCs:

A. Acknowledge him. Let him know you're thinking about him. "Hi, Lord. I love you. Would you go into my day with me?"

B. Bring it. Tell him about your concerns or needs. "Lord, I'm worried about making rent this month. Would you show me what to do? Would you provide for my need?"

C. Chat. Tell God whatever is on your mind. For example, you could tell him about your day, problems, job, family, bank account, or mother-in-law, just as if you were talking to a good friend. "Lord, did you see the family at dinner tonight? I'm worried about little Bobby. He seemed so quiet, and I'm wondering if something's wrong. Would you comfort him and give me wisdom to know how to talk to him about what's going on?"

Whatever you bring to God, he'll help you through. Then when you look back, you'll see his fingerprints on the things you brought to him in prayer.

Sure, God already knows everything about whatever topic you might bring up, but that's not the point. The point is, just like in any relationship, you need to communicate because communication builds intimacy. Don't be afraid of saying the wrong thing because God already knows your heart. God is big enough to take your joy, your tears, your fear, your frustrations, your anger, and even your tantrums. But what he doesn't want from you is a cold shoulder. Whatever you bring to God, he'll help you through. Then when you look back, you'll see his fingerprints on the things you brought to him in prayer.

Let's stop and practice this kind of communication right now. Out loud, in writing, or in a whisper in your heart, pray.

Acknowledge him

_____

_____

Bring it

_____

_____

Chat

_____

_____

_____

Perhaps you felt a little uncomfortable doing this exercise. If you practice these prayer ABCs daily, you will find that praying will get a lot easier and you will begin to enjoy a fresh closeness with God.

Prayer, the Power to Transform Us

God has the power to transform your circumstances, but more importantly, God has the power to transform you. Author Stormie Omartian says:

It's no wonder that we aren't able to change ourselves. We don't even understand what we are to be changed to or why. Only God can open our eyes to see these things. That's why we have to pray the "Change me, Lord, prayer." I know it's one of the most frightening and difficult prayers to pray. . . . But there is a way we can pray that will change us, and it's not frightening. That is to pray, "Make me more like Christ."[3]

> *God has the power to transform your circumstances, but more importantly, God has the power to transform you.*

Stormie's prayer is awesome, and I recommend you pray it now.

Change me, Lord. Make me more like you.

Just like deciding to pray the above prayer, building intimacy with God is a choice we make. We do not choose whether or not God sent his Son to redeem us, but we choose whether or not to accept that gift. It's been said that we can have as much of God in our lives as we want. Another way of saying it is that we can choose whether or not to allow God to move in our lives and to transform us into the person he created us to be.

> *We can choose whether or not to allow God to move in our lives and to transform us into the person he created us to be.*

Our transformation starts with our initial choice to believe in God. Even if our understanding of God isn't perfectly clear, we have to say, "Yes, I choose to believe." In fact, before my husband came to faith, he came to that very conclusion. As an eighteen-year-old physics major who studied mathematical equations that explain what is known about the universe, he was on a personal quest to discover if God was real. In those days, as I was one of his believing friends, he'd often call me late at night to question me about God. But nothing I said could absolutely convince him that God was real. Then one night, Paul came to the conclusion, "I have to make a choice to believe or not."

Later, he told me, "I chose to believe. I decided to give it everything."

Paul made that decision without the absolute proof he'd sought. But today, over thirty years later, he's even more convinced that God is real. His decision to believe removed the veil that blinded him.

The veil of blindness may not lift until we choose to believe. It's like the story of Moses, who, after spending time with God, so glowed with the glory of God that the people asked him to wear a veil. But listen to the point that the apostle Paul, himself a Jew, made about the veil that separates so many from God.

Not only Moses' face was veiled, but his people's minds and understanding were veiled and blinded too. Even now when the Scripture is read it seems as though Jewish hearts and minds are covered by a thick veil, because they cannot see and understand the real meaning of the Scriptures. For this veil of misunderstanding can be removed only by believing in Christ. Yes, even today when they read Moses' writings their hearts are blind and they think that obeying the Ten Commandments is the way to be saved.

But whenever anyone turns to the Lord from his sins, then the veil is taken away. The Lord is the Spirit who gives them life, and where he is there is freedom [from trying to be saved by keeping the laws of God]. But we Christians have no veil over our faces; we can be mirrors that brightly reflect the glory

> *God will even transform our weaknesses into strengths, if we will allow him, for transformation is a continuing process, one we can choose to continue, to stall, or even to reject.*

of the Lord. And as the Spirit of the Lord works within us, we become more and more like him. (2 Cor. 3:14–18 TLB)

God wants us to reflect his glory as we become more like him. This transformation starts the moment we first believe. God will even transform our weaknesses into strengths, if we will allow him, for transformation is a continuing process, one we can choose to continue, to stall, or even to reject.

Choose to Receive God's Best for You

Imagine a five-year-old with his nose pressed to the window of a bakery filled with giant iced cookies, incredible fruit-filled tarts, and warm and gooey cinnamon buns fresh from the oven. As the boy stares at these wonders, his loving father gives his shoulder a squeeze. "Son, would you like to go in?"

The lad nods and follows as his daddy pushes open the shop's door. The bell jingles, and the smell of fresh-baked bread welcomes them. The father reaches for an empty pastry box and hands it to his son. "Pick out whatever you like."

Stunned, the boy stares up at this dad, then looks through the glass at the shelves full of delights.

But instead of pointing to his favorite, the chocolate éclair bursting with sweet vanilla cream and topped with a cherry, the boy turns away, his chin to his chest. Surely his father didn't really mean he could have whatever he wanted. This promise was too good to be true. These wonderful baked goods *must* be for others, not for him.

As he stares at the floor, he sees crumbs, old wrappers, chocolate-smeared napkins, and even bits of dried leaves that blew in when they opened the door. So instead of choosing the creamiest treats, the lad fills his box with stale crumbs and trash.

What a crazy story!

But as crazy as it may seem, we are just like this boy. We've seen what God promises us in the Bible, promises such as forgiveness, transformation, and grace. But we find these promises difficult to believe. Oh, we can believe these wonderful delights are available for others, but for us? Hasn't God seen our bad attitude? Didn't he hear when we lost our temper or spoke harshly to our neighbor? We cannot sample the delights he offers because all we deserve is crumbs.

Are you kidding me? We are talking about a God who loves us unconditionally, a God who is filled with mercy and grace. He's not saying, "You can sample my blessings when you're good enough." No! His Son's very blood covers our

---

We are talking about a God who loves us unconditionally, a God who is filled with mercy and grace. He's not saying, "You can sample my blessings when you're good enough." No! His Son's very blood covers our sin and makes us good enough.

---

sin and makes us good enough. Do we believe Christ died on the cross for nothing? Do we now have to earn our way to God's forgiveness, transformation, and grace?

The real deal is that forgiveness, transformation, and grace belong to us, if we would but choose to receive.

Behold Jesus

As the sun began to slide west of the little village of Bethany, Mary found herself hard at work, pushing stubby sticks into the fire inside their jar-like oven, which had been dug into the center of the kitchen. She wiped the sweat from her brow and asked her sister, "What time will the men arrive?"

Martha looked up from chopping the garlic and leeks, which she was about to stir into the steaming lentil and mutton stew. "You know how unpredictable that brother of ours is. He could arrive anytime now or even well after dark."

Mary sighed, knowing her sister's words were true. But when the smell of baking bread caught Mary's attention, she quickly turned and retrieved a freshly browned loaf from the oven's open mouth. As she admired the loaf, she imagined the moment when the young rabbi Jesus would bless and break it at their dinner table.

Mary loved not only the way Jesus blessed bread but also the way he blessed people. In the market, she'd seen Jesus open the eyes of Admon, the blind beggar. The women who gathered daily at the local well still marveled over the miracle, mainly because the miracle continued. In fact, just that very morning, as Mary and Martha had hurried to the market with their shopping list, they'd passed Admon as he strolled down the road toward the vineyards. Now that Admon's eyesight had returned, he no longer begged in the market but worked alongside his brother to pluck the ripest grapes for the village's winepress. It was even rumored that he would soon take a wife. Mary's heart rejoiced at the wonder of it!

Not only did Jesus open the eyes of the blind, but his teachings also provoked her to consider the power of loving God. It was only an afternoon ago that Mary had stood beneath the shade of a sycamore tree and heard Jesus say, "Love the Lord with all your heart, soul, and strength, and love your neighbor as yourself." This was a lesson she now tried to apply to all she did.

Mary hummed one of David's psalms of worship as she thought of the night's gathering. There were so many questions she wanted to ask Jesus, like, "Are you the promised Messiah?"

Just as Mary started to slice her freshly baked fig cakes, the front door opened and Mary could hear the men enter their home. She and Martha exchanged panicked glances. Lazarus was early!

Mary paused to peek through the kitchen door, and there he was—Jesus.

There was something about the way he turned and smiled at her, not in a romantic sort of way but in a way that spoke of God's love for her very soul. Mary couldn't help herself. She pulled off her apron, wiped the flour from her hands, and slipped into the room as Jesus began to tell those gathered around him, "The Kingdom of Heaven can be compared to a woman making bread. She takes a measure of flour and mixes in the yeast until it permeates every part of the dough."[4]

Mary closed her eyes in delight. It was so like Jesus to teach through a story, but it was a story she understood. Yeast transforms the dough, but could the kingdom of God transform her life the same way?

As she contemplated this, the kitchen door swung open, and there stood Martha with a fist balled into one of her ample hips. She pointed at Mary as she said, "Jesus, do you not care that my sister has left me to serve alone? Tell her to get back into the kitchen to help me."

Mary's cheeks felt hot. She started to rise from her spot on the floor, but when she glanced at the Master, he shook his head and motioned for her to stay. He turned to Martha and gently admonished, "Martha, Martha, you are so worried and troubled about many things. But Mary has chosen that which is best, and it will not be taken away from her."

Martha's eyes suddenly glistened as her anger melted. She quickly disappeared into the kitchen, returning shortly with the warm bread, lentil stew, fig cakes, and dewy grapes, which they had so lovingly prepared.

Mary felt proud of Martha as she watched her sister present the meal to their guests. She was glad when Martha sat at the feet of Jesus herself, listening to his teaching. Jesus's words were powerful that night, and Mary knew that because she had chosen the best gift, those words would forever stay in her heart (based on Luke 10:39–42).

What exactly did Mary choose? Mary chose to behold Jesus.

When we behold Jesus, we are transformed to become more like him. We discover the kingdom of heaven, and we have more love, joy, peace, patience, as well as a better realization of God's abiding presence in our lives.

In my book *When You Need a Miracle: How to Ask God for the Impossible*, I share a list of attributes that describe our transformation.[5] In Christ:

> You are loved: "For God so loved the world that he gave his one and only Son, that whoever believes in him shall not perish but have eternal life." (John 3:16)

You are forgiven: "I am writing to you, dear children, because your sins have been forgiven on account of his name." (1 John 2:12)

You are righteous: "God made him who had no sin to be sin for us, so that in him we might become the righteousness of God." (2 Cor. 5:21)

You are justified: "All are justified freely by his grace through the redemption that came by Christ Jesus." (Rom. 3:24)

You are in Christ: "God raised us up with Christ and seated us with him in the heavenly realms in Christ Jesus." (Eph. 2:6)

Christ is in you: "To them God has chosen to make known among the Gentiles the glorious riches of this mystery, which is Christ in you, the hope of glory." (Col. 1:27)

> *Behold Jesus, meditate on his every word, and enjoy his presence as he transforms you to be more like him.*

You are not condemned: "Therefore, there is now no condemnation for those who are in Christ Jesus." (Rom. 8:1)

You are an overcomer: "You, dear children, are from God and have overcome them, because the one who is in you is greater than the one who is in the world." (1 John 4:4)

You are more than a conqueror: "In all these things we are more than conquerors through him who loved us." (Rom. 8:37)

You are a victor: "For everyone born of God overcomes the world. This is the victory that has overcome the world, even our faith." (1 John 5:4)

Stop for a moment to consider that these ten descriptors now apply to you.

Beholding Jesus in Prayer

Don't let anyone shoo you away from choosing the best part. Behold Jesus, meditate on his every word, and enjoy his presence as he transforms you to be more like him.

Author Adrian Warnock writes, "The more we gaze upon the risen, gloried King Jesus, the more we will become like him. The more we see Jesus for who he is, the more we will be made into his image. . . . Ultimately there will be a day when we will see Jesus face-to-face, and in an instant our transformation will be complete."[6]

Dear Lord,

It's my goal to learn how to see you, to behold you so that you will transform me to be more like you. Just as you did not shoo Mary back to the kitchen, neither do you shoo me from sitting at your feet to soak in the knowledge of your presence or to experience it as I read your Word.

As I start to see myself through you, I see that I am loved, forgiven, righteous, justified, in you, not condemned, an overcomer, more than a conqueror, and a victor. I also see that you are in me. That's a pretty wonderful list.

As I take my eyes off myself and look at you, I see you are gazing into my soul with pure love. Teach me how to meet your gaze, no matter what is happening in my life, for the more I behold you, the less of a grip my issues, such as my past, present, or future, will have

*over me. Everything will fall away like broken chains.
In Jesus's name, amen.*

Listening Prayer

One of the best ways to behold Jesus and to continue a conversation with God is to spend time meditating on his Word,
something we'll do right now.

1. First, ask God to quiet your mind and to speak to you.
   Then read Romans 12:2 (NKJV):

   And do not be conformed to this world, but be transformed by the renewing of your mind, that you may
   prove what is that good and acceptable and perfect will
   of God.

2. Next, read these verses again, slowly, and write down
   thoughts that occur to you. Then read them again, emphasizing different words or phrases. Then write down
   any more thoughts that occur to you.

   _____

   _____

   _____

   _____

   _____

   _____

   _____

3. Read over what you have written to discern if God is
   speaking to you. You may hear from him right away,

or you may have to continue to practice this listening prayer as you continue to meditate on his Word.

Making It Personal

Dear Lord,

It's so exciting to spend this time with you as I contemplate your Word. As I do, you transform me to be more like you, and I see how you see me: loved, forgiven, covered in your mercy and grace, with your very Spirit in me. As I spend time with you, show me your will and how to live. Help me to reflect your glory in a way that will draw others to you like a moth to a flame. In Jesus's name, amen.

3

Experience God's Blessings

How we praise God, the Father of our Lord Jesus Christ, who has blessed us with every blessing in heaven because we belong to Christ.

Ephesians 1:3 TLB

Would you feel better about your life if you could find blessings hiding inside your disappointments?

You can!

I had some time to contemplate this truth last Saturday afternoon at a local coffee shop. After getting coffee, I hopped in my car and shifted into reverse. I pulled out of my space, but when I tried to put my car into drive, a sudden pop vibrated through the steering column, and I was stuck in park. No matter what I tried, nothing worked. My car was immovable as it sat blocking the parking lot's traffic lane.

Rattled and embarrassed by the cars that were forming a line behind me, I climbed out of my car and waved them around. After the line cleared, I walked over and sat down at one of the iron grill tables outside the coffee shop and called my husband on my cell phone. "I'll be there in twenty," he told me.

There I sat staring at my lovely silver car, which had so faithfully served me for the last eleven years. In many ways, it was like a time capsule filled with memories of driving my kids around. It even had pockets still stuffed with old, abandoned toys that had once belonged to my son, now a college senior. So with a heavy heart, I sat in my chair, an iced mocha in front of me, watching the drivers maneuver around my car.

A feeling of God's presence settled on me, and I suddenly noticed the amazing blue of the August sky and realized that the afternoon breeze felt refreshingly cool. "How blessed I am, Lord, to have a breakdown in such a safe place. Thank you," I prayed as I took another sip of my iced mocha and bit into my peanut butter cookie. "And look, you even provided refreshments!"

Just then, another driver pulled up, a woman in a white suburban. I wasn't sure she saw that I was waving at her to pull around, so I stood up. When I did, she lowered her window and leaned over to inquire, "Is there a dead body inside that car? I've been trying to see the driver, but I can't."

"No," I called back, smiling. "The only thing that's dead is the car."

She drove around, and I chuckled, telling the Lord, "See, Lord, it could have been a lot worse; there are no dead bodies in my car."

I sat down, and two women walked out of the coffee shop. "Is that your car?" one of the women asked.

"Yes," I said. "It broke down. My hubby's on the way."

The other woman said, "I love your attitude. Here you sit with your car broken down, smiling and waving at people, and sipping coffee as if you were a queen entertaining guests."

"Just counting my blessings," I said. "Just think, I could have been at the airport on my way to catch a plane, or I could have been in the middle of a busy intersection, but here I am in a safe place enjoying a peanut butter cookie."

"And who knows," the first one said, "you might even get a new car out of the deal."

We all laughed at that idea.

Soon my husband pulled into the parking lot, and I got to spend the rest of the afternoon with him on a much-needed "date." Of course, the date was spent directing traffic around my car and securing a tow truck, but even so, we had a lovely time together. And the best news is, though I'm not getting a new car, the repair bill for the broken cable in my steering column was minimal and the cost of the tow was covered under my AAA plan.

How blessed I am!

I told you this story to say that though we can't control the things that happen to us, we can recognize that God is with us and we can watch for his blessings even in the uninvited happenstances of life.

In fact, it seems that blessings multiply when we:

- count them
- discover how Jesus wants to bless us
- become a blessing

Dear Lord,

Thank you that you are with me even on grouchy days or grumpy mornings. You are with me even when the kids fight, the dogs bite, or hurts sting. You are with me in boring meetings, difficult commutes, financial woes, and my own angry or worried silences. So I ask, Lord, that during these and other difficult times you would open my eyes to your presence and remind me of all your abundant blessings. Teach me to count them, discover more of them, and become a blessing myself. In Jesus's name, amen.

Count Our Blessings

I came across a delightful quotation from country singing star Willie Nelson. He said, "When I started counting my blessings, my whole life turned around."[1]

Look at it this way. As you read my story about my broken-down car, you could have thought, *Ha! Linda thinks she's blessed in her petty little car crisis. She doesn't know what a real crisis is!*

> *"When I started counting my blessings, my whole life turned around."*

Yes, I hear the pain out there, but let me tell you how I would have told my car story if I hadn't realized God's presence that afternoon.

Can you believe it? I'd left my house only for a minute because goodness knows my book deadline was breathing down my neck. All I needed was a cup of coffee so I could hurry home and write. And of course, my car would break down in front of the coffee shop, blocking the traffic in a parking lot. Can you imagine? All I wanted was a little cup of coffee, and what I got instead was a big hassle. Not a private hassle. Oh no, my car had to inconvenience all the other drivers. How embarrassing! Someone even thought there was a dead body in my car.

Anyway, my husband, who also had a busy afternoon planned, had to drop everything and babysit me while we waited for a tow. By the time the ordeal was over, five hours had passed, and I was too tired to write a word. What a wasted day.

Wow, that was a negative stream of thoughts, and, I'll admit, it would have been easy for me to slip into negativity if I had let a bad attitude shut God out of my experience. There were days I might have pushed God out of my uninvited difficulties and chalked the day up as a wasted day—instead of a day filled with blessings. So what made the difference for me? My change of heart began the moment I recognized God's presence. Acknowledging his presence made it easier for me to make a conscious effort to thank him as I counted my blessings.

With this in mind, let's evaluate the following message someone once received from the food stamp program. The letter, in part, read, "Your food stamps will be stopped effective March 2013 because we received notice that you passed away. May God bless you. You may reapply if there is a change in your circumstances."

Wait a minute. Is this a good notice or a bad notice? Well, it depends. If you really did pass away and are now with Jesus, then you don't need food stamps, and so there's a blessing in that. But if you didn't pass away, why be upset? You got a governmental agency to give you a blessing and a chance to reapply for their program.

Author and illustrator Karla Dornacher once wrote:

> God is love, and every gift he gives is a perfect expression of his loving nature. He doesn't bless you out of duty. He blesses you because he wants to. He loves you and showers you with gifts of every kind. Spiritual. Physical. Mental. Emotional. Relational. If you were to write a list of God's blessings, it would truly be never ending, for every breath you take . . . every moment of your life is a gift![2]

If "the secret to happiness is to count your blessings while others are adding up their troubles,"[3] then let me lead you in a little exercise. Take some time to revisit a recent difficulty in your life. As you think about it, try to envision the fact that God's loving presence was with you, getting you through. Write down a few of his blessings regarding your new perspective on your difficulty:

1. _____

2. _____

3. _____

4. _____

5. _____

Did this exercise help you discover any unnoticed blessings? Let's take some time to go to the Lord in prayer.

Dear Lord,

Thank you that you are with me, even when I am not aware of it. Open my eyes and help me to be more aware of you. As my awareness of you grows, help me to see that because you love me you are constantly leaving me blessings, even in the midst of my troubles. Help me to view my life in such a way that I gather your blessings like a bouquet of flowers from you to me. Help me to remember that you are getting me through. In Jesus's name, amen.

Discover the Blessings Jesus Gave Us

The opening Scripture passage in this chapter, Ephesians 1:3, states, "How we praise God, the Father of our Lord Jesus

Christ, who has blessed us with every blessing in heaven because we belong to Christ" (TLB).

What wonderful news, especially when we also consider Psalm 73:21–24, which says, "When I was beleaguered and bitter, totally consumed by envy, I was totally ignorant, a dumb ox in your very presence. I'm still in your presence, but you've taken my hand. You wisely and tenderly lead me, and then you bless me" (Message).

These Scripture passages reveal that we have a God who both blesses and guides us, even before we pay attention to the fact that he is with us. To help us pay attention to both God and his blessings, let's take a look at the Beatitudes, Jesus's summary of how we should live:

> God blesses those who are poor and realize their need
> for him,
>   for the Kingdom of Heaven is theirs.
> God blesses those who mourn,
>   for they will be comforted.
> God blesses those who are humble,
>   for they will inherit the whole earth.
> God blesses those who hunger and thirst for justice,
>   for they will be satisfied.
> God blesses those who are merciful,
>   for they will be shown mercy.
> God blesses those whose hearts are pure,
>   for they will see God.
> God blesses those who work for peace,
>   for they will be called the children of God.
> God blesses those who are persecuted for doing right,
>   for the Kingdom of Heaven is theirs.

God blesses you when people mock you and persecute you and lie about you and say all sorts of evil things against you because you are my followers. Be happy about it! Be very glad!

For a great reward awaits you in heaven. And remember, the ancient prophets were persecuted in the same way. (Matt. 5:3–12 NLT)

What powerful words from Jesus, words that teach us we are blessed when we realize how much we need God, mourn, are humble, are hungry and thirsty for justice, are merciful, are pure in heart, work for peace, are persecuted for doing right, and are mocked, persecuted, lied about, or slandered because we are Christ's followers.

> When we live for God, he flips our struggles into miracles of blessings, either on this side of heaven or in eternity.

In many ways, Jesus is saying, when you live for me, even when you are in lack or even when living for me costs you something, I will bless you with many good gifts, including comfort, a wonderful inheritance in Christ, satisfaction, mercy, the ability to see God, being called God's child, inheriting the kingdom of heaven, and having a great reward in heaven.

In other words, when we live for God, he flips our struggles into miracles of blessings, either on this side of heaven or in eternity.

Dear Lord,

I praise you, God the Father of our Lord Jesus Christ. You have blessed me with every blessing in heaven because I belong to Christ! Thank you for blessing me, even in trouble. You gently guide me, even when I stand before your presence ignorant as an ox. Help me to be more mindful of you and the blessings you have for me even in my difficulties, for you promise that when

I realize my need for you, the kingdom of heaven is mine. You promise that when I mourn, you will comfort me, when I am humble, I will inherit the whole earth, and when I am hungry and thirsty for justice, I will be satisfied. Thank you.

God, you will bless me with mercy when I am merciful, you will help me see you when my heart is pure, you will call me your child when I work for peace, you will bless me by giving me entrance into the kingdom of heaven when I am persecuted for doing right. You will bless me when others mock, persecute, lie about, or slander me because I am your follower, for you say that great is my reward in heaven.

Thank you, Lord, for both earthly and heavenly blessings. In Jesus's name, amen.

Become a Blessing

After studying the Beatitudes, I would have to agree with the statement that the person who learns to be a blessing to others is indeed blessed. Even Jesus said, "It is more blessed to give than to receive" (Acts 20:35 KJV).

When I was being interviewed on the radio the other day, a caller asked, "How do you classify a circumstance in which a person asks God for something and then another person actually fulfills the request? Would you call that a miracle?

I answered, "Yes, because Christ lives in our hearts. Therefore, we are his living representation here on earth. So when we feel impressed to do a kindness, we should do it, because the Holy Spirit impresses us to do it."

Then I told him a story. "There was a couple who had no money to buy gas for their car but felt God was calling them to drive to church. If they went, they would not have enough gas to get back home. After praying about it, they felt God was leading them to go to church anyway. On the way home from church, the husband felt God was leading them to stop at the gas pump even though they had no money to pay for gas. When he opened the car's gas cap, he found a folded fifty dollar bill tucked neatly inside the cap.

When we feel impressed to do a kindness, we should do it, because the Holy Spirit impresses us to do it.

"How did it get there? God had impressed a gentleman from the church, who did not know about the family's financial crisis, to place that fifty dollar bill in the gas cap.

"Was that a miracle? Yes! God used this kind gentleman to act as his hands and feet to help answer a prayer!"

Let me encourage you not only to pray for miracles but also to ask God to help you *become* a miracle. Then listen up and follow his lead. Just remember to use your safety net, which is this: God will never call you to do anything that goes against his Word.

Let me encourage you not only to pray for miracles but also to ask God to help you become a miracle.

> Dear Lord,
> I long not only for blessings in my life but also to be a blessing and to be used by you to reach out and help others. Open my eyes to you. Tune my inner ear to your Holy Spirit. Take me on adventures so that I become your hands and feet. Help me to overcome fear as I do all that you call me to do—to be a blessing to others. In Jesus's name, amen.

Behold Jesus

If you've ever felt invisible, insignificant, or unworthy of God's blessings, perhaps you will relate to the story of Jesus blessing the children, as told through the eyes of a child who thought no one noticed her.

There were days when five-year-old Sara felt invisible. Her mother always had the baby on her hip, and her brothers said she was too little to follow them on their adventures around the city. Plus, her father was too busy earning the family's living to pay attention to her.

So when Sara, her mother, and her siblings ventured out to see Jesus beneath the shady sycamore tree one afternoon, her mother pushed the boys forward. "Master, will you bless my children?" she asked.

Sara watched as Jesus's disciples tried to shoo her brothers away. "Can't you see how busy the Master is?" the one called Peter asked.

But Jesus would have none of it. He sat down on a nearby rock and opened his arms wide. "Do not forbid the children to come to me," he told his disciples.

Sara looked at him, wide-eyed from behind her mother's skirts, certain that Jesus hadn't even noticed her, such an insignificant little girl. But Jesus's smile was wide, and he opened his arms even wider. Sara looked up at her mom, who nodded.

Then, with a rush and a leap, Sara was in his arms as Jesus finished his sentence. "For the kingdom of heaven belongs to such as these."

Jesus put his hand on her head and sweetly blessed her, just as he did her brothers. That's when Sara knew she was no longer insignificant. She was blessed, because Jesus had said so (based on Matt. 19:13–14).

You are not invisible or insignificant to Jesus. He loves you and is waiting for you to notice that his blessings are also for you. You are blessed, because Jesus says so.

Beholding Jesus in Prayer

What about you? Do you have a hard time believing that Jesus has placed his hand on your head and sweetly blessed you?

He has blessed you. You are not invisible or insignificant to Jesus. He loves you and is waiting for you to notice that his blessings are also for you. You are blessed, because Jesus says so.

> *Dear Lord,*
> *Thank you that you see me and that your arms are open wide to me. Thank you that your blessing is also for me, for I come to you like a little child—trusting in your love and care for me. In Jesus's name, amen.*

Listening Prayer

Rejoice! You are blessed by God.

1. First, ask God to quiet your mind and to speak to you. Then read Ephesians 1:3–12 (TLB):

> How we praise God, the Father of our Lord Jesus Christ, who has blessed us with every blessing in heaven because we belong to Christ.

Long ago, even before he made the world, God chose us to be his very own, through what Christ would do for us; he decided then to make us holy in his eyes, without a single fault—we who stand before him covered with his love. His unchanging plan has always been to adopt us into his own family by sending Jesus Christ to die for us. And he did this because he wanted to!

Now all praise to God for his wonderful kindness to us and his favor that he has poured out upon us, because we belong to his dearly loved Son. So overflowing is his kindness towards us that he took away all our sins through the blood of his Son, by whom we are saved; and he has showered down upon us the richness of his grace—for how well he understands us and knows what is best for us at all times.

God has told us his secret reason for sending Christ, a plan he decided on in mercy long ago; and this was his purpose: that when the time is ripe he will gather us all together from wherever we are—in heaven or on earth—to be with him in Christ, forever. Moreover, because of what Christ has done we have become gifts to God that he delights in, for as part of God's sovereign plan we were chosen from the beginning to be his, and all things happen just as he decided long ago. God's purpose in this was that we should praise God and give glory to him for doing these mighty things for us, who were the first to trust in Christ.

2. Next, read these verses again, slowly, and write down thoughts that occur to you. Then read them again, emphasizing different words or phrases. Then write down any more thoughts that occur to you.

_____

_____

_____

_____

_____

_____

_____

3. Read over what you have written to discern if God is speaking to you. You may hear from him right away, or you may have to continue to practice this listening prayer as you continue to meditate on his Word.

Making It Personal

Dear Lord,

I am blessed! Christ purchased the grace that I now wear as I stand before you as your very own child, in a robe of pure love.

I know I was bought at a great price and fully belong to you because of the shed blood of Christ. I'm thankful that you know what is best for me all the time. Because of your gift of grace to me, I am now a gift to you. Therefore, I bless your holy name.

One day, I will be gathered together with all your sons and daughters and will be with you in glory. Praise your name, forevermore. In Jesus's name, amen.

4

Experience God's Hope

May the God of hope fill you with all joy and peace as you
trust in him, so that you may overflow with hope by the power
of the Holy Spirit.

Romans 15:13

What do you do when you've lost hope?
Last Memorial Day, I experienced that sickening
feeling.

My hubby decided to ride his bicycle over the Vail Mountain Pass and down into the ski town of Vail, Colorado, and
we agreed that I would drive our truck over to meet him for
lunch.

When I got to Vail, I steered our truck into a dimly lit
parking garage, passing through long rows of cars. Then,
just before the first turn, I found what looked like the perfect
parking spot and pulled in. I hopped out of the truck and
looked around, and though I didn't see a sign telling me my
level and location, I noted that I was at the very end of the

garage just next to a corner door. *This parking spot will be a cinch to find when I return*, I decided and slipped out of the garage to walk across the covered bridge and into town.

Later, after having an iced tea and a grilled chicken sandwich at a restaurant near the river, I waved good-bye to Paul, who'd hopped back on his bike to make the return trip. I crossed the covered bridge and returned to the Vail parking garage. But once inside, it was as if our truck had vanished.

Maybe I'm on the wrong level, I thought, so I quickly located a nearby elevator and got off on each floor. Though I searched thoroughly, I had no luck on levels one or two, and when the door opened onto level three, I was shocked by what I saw: a bartender wiping down a bar. What had happened to the parking garage?

I found a woman working at a nearby desk, but she had no idea how to help me find my truck, so I returned to the elevator and continued to explore every nook of the garage, both inside and out. After searching for two more hours, I suddenly remembered a little statistic about Memorial Day. It's the day when more cars are stolen in the United States than any other day.

My heart sank. Oh no!

Finally, back on level two, I walked over to an empty parking space, the very spot where I believed I'd left the truck. I sighed deeply and stared at an oil stain on the pavement. I was exhausted, I had no place left to search, and I had lost hope that I would see my truck again. In my despair, I decided to call on God one last time. Can you please help me?

Next, I did what I'd already done a hundred times. I pressed the alarm button on my key. In that eerie moment, the truck's horn suddenly blared. The honking was so loud that you'd think I was standing on top of the truck, but yet it was nowhere to be seen.

I pressed the button again, and the honking stopped. Then I pressed it once more, and the frantic honking resumed. What was going on?

That's when I spied what appeared to be a broom closet tucked behind some water pipes just to my right. There on the door was a tiny sign that simply read "stairs." I pushed open the door and took the steps two at a time, following the sound of my blaring horn. When I banged through the door labeled "level 3," I did not see a bar but a group of people gathered around my honking truck. The people turned and stared at me, a wild-eyed woman who had just popped out of a secret passage in a parking garage.

It was a sterling moment for us all. But I was thrilled to be reunited with my truck and very glad I hadn't called the police to report it missing. A call like that would have put me in the police notes of the Vail newspaper: "Prayer author lost all hope of finding her truck in our city's parking garage and called us. We found her truck in three seconds."

Since that day, I've learned that this garage is notorious for losing cars, which, come to think of it, is probably how that bar stays in business.

But joking aside, losing hope is no laughing matter.

Recently, I did a call-in radio interview in Smyrna Beach, Florida, where the hostess told me, "I'm so glad you're going to be on my show today because there are so many hurting people here, especially with the space center closing. A lot of folks have just lost hope."

Losing hope seems to be a common problem in the world today. I've heard so many stories. "My husband left me." "I can't get a job." "My unemployment ran out." "I'm desperate." "The doctor gave no hope." "I'm chronically depressed." "I can't stop drinking . . . doing drugs . . . self-harming." "I'm already dead."

Heartbreaking!

And when you're in a situation like one of these, it's hard to imagine that God—the one you've pleaded with, poured out your heart to—even cares. (Or else why hasn't he fixed your situation?)

When your hope is waning, it's difficult to find your way through your problem-filled maze to a solution. So what should you do? You need to:

• keep seeking God
• choose to hope
• take the next step

Let's take a moment to pray before we continue to ponder the puzzle of hope.

Dear Lord,

In times of loss and confusion, it's hard to understand why you don't just change my circumstances. In fact, Lord, sometimes I feel like I'm lost in an endless maze. But yet I know you are bigger than my problems, and despite my confusion about what to do next, I know you are not lost—you will guide me to where I need to be. That's why I choose to stick with you. Give me strength, Lord, your strength. In Jesus's name, amen.

Keep Seeking God

Maybe you are unwavering in your quest to seek God, or maybe like a lot of people you are thinking, *Seeking God sounds like a great idea, except for one thing. God is mad at me. The last thing I want to do is draw attention to myself by coming out of hiding.*

62

God knows you're not perfect and that you sometimes fail. He even knows that some of your failures may have contributed to your troubles, but nevertheless, God loves you.

Wait a minute. God knows you're not perfect and that you sometimes fail. He even knows that some of your failures may have contributed to your troubles, but nevertheless, God loves you. He wants to lead you, teach you, and even take your failures and turn them into redeemed purposes, if you'll let him.

But perhaps, like Adam and Eve, you feel that moving closer to a holy God will give your imperfections too much exposure. I understand your concern, as none of us is perfect. But despite your failures, there's no need for embarrassment. You are God's beloved child—a child he does not want to harm but wants to prosper, as Jeremiah 29:11 says: "'For I know the plans I have for you,' declares the LORD, 'plans to prosper you and not to harm you, plans to give you hope and a future.'"

If you can start to trust that God's intentions toward you are good, then perhaps you can relax in his presence and realize that his grace, love, and care are even for you. When you begin to accept this truth, perhaps you will better understand Romans 8:1, which says, "So now there is no condemnation for those who belong to Christ Jesus" (NLT).

The problem is when your focus becomes your failures and self-judgments. Then you will perceive God as angry instead of loving. But when you focus on God's forgiveness and grace, you will find it easier to walk in God's love. You will be inspired to become a better person.

> *When you focus on God's forgiveness and grace, you will find it easier to walk in God's love.*

Sometimes hopelessness comes not through personal failures but through unexplainable difficulties and heartaches. When it does, you can still focus on God and his great love. Regardless of why you are struggling with hope, call out to him in prayer.

Dear Lord,

I come out of hiding and stand before you, not in terror but in grace, because Jesus Christ has covered my sins with his righteousness. Help me to stop focusing on my shortcomings and instead to focus on your goodness and grace. Yes, I admit to my failures, but you have hidden them in Christ Jesus and have forgiven me. How can I thank you for such a gift?

I ask that you guide me through the pitfalls of hopelessness and into a bright tomorrow of hope and purpose. Thank you that I can relax in your love for me and even give you my fear of tomorrow. Thank you that you are the giver of hope and that you are giving this gift to me. In Jesus's name, amen.

Choose to Hope

When you think about it, hope is a choice. It's something you can give up or something you can cling to.

"In all of my trials, it has become quite clear that I have a choice," says army chaplain wife Rebekah Benimoff.

I could take all my pain and grief and unanswered questions and truthfully, honestly submit them to El Shaddai, "The God Who is Sufficient for His People," or I could choose to turn away from Him and become resentful. I could choose Hope—or I could choose to walk away from hope.

Hope is a choice. It's something you can give up or something you can cling to.

How could I choose hopelessness when there is such HOPE to be found? I find myself crying out to Him saying, "God, I cannot do this on my own. I choose hope despite what I cannot understand. I choose to believe God is who he says he is, despite what my circumstances are."[1]

Do you know what's so great about clinging to hope? Hope is like a strong cord, a lifeline that stretches straight from God to you. The more you choose to cling to it, the more you are transferring the weight of your burdens to God. Depression and desperation vanish as you continue to cling to hope.

Also consider that hope helps set your faith in motion, as described in Hebrews 11:1: "Faith is the confidence that what we hope for will actually happen; it gives us assurance about things we cannot see" (NLT). So take the advice in

Hope is like a strong cord, a lifeline that stretches straight from God to you. The more you choose to cling to it, the more you are transferring the weight of your burdens to God.

Romans 12:12: "Be joyful in hope, patient in affliction, faithful in prayer."

The reason you should be joyful in hope is because God, even when he seems to wait until the last minute to move, always gets the last word. It's as 1 Peter 5:10–11 explains:

> Keep your guard up. You're not the only ones plunged into these hard times. It's the same with Christians all over the world. So keep a firm grip on the faith. The suffering won't last forever. It won't be long before this generous God who has great plans for us in Christ—eternal and glorious plans they are!—will have you put together and on your feet for good. He gets the last word; yes, he does. (Message)

Dear Lord,

Neither the enemy nor my problems get the last word about my life. You do! I know that though it often seems you wait until the last moment, your timing is perfect.

I chose to hope in you, for you were not sent to punish me but to be my Redeemer.

Thank you that I can hope in you. In Jesus's name, amen.

Take the Next Step

Pastor and author Ray Pritchard once asked:

> Does God have a blueprint that includes everything in your life from the moment of your birth to the moment of your death? . . . The answer to that question is yes. But the only part of it you can see arrives each morning in the form of twenty-four brand-new hours, freshly delivered by United Angel Service Overnight Express. Please don't miss the point: God wants to teach us to trust him step by step. He reveals

his will one step at a time, so we can trust him moment by moment.[2]

But where does God promise that his blueprint for your life will be easy to follow?

Even when things are going according to God's plan, there may be days when you'll need to take cover from the flaming arrows of discouragement, depression, fear, or confusion. The best way to extinguish these arrows is to rejoice that God has given us weapons of warfare (2 Cor. 10:4) and that he has delivered us from the power of darkness (Col. 1:13).

It's good to know that we don't have to live under the dominion of the enemy. But though we will get everything we need, we may not get everything we want. Pritchard puts it this way: "Doing God's will means taking the next step—whatever it is—without a definite promise about the end result."[3]

> *Following the will of God will always result in unexpected miracles.*

What we do know about God's will is this: God's will is for us to be kind, to be more like Jesus, and to do good things that will draw more people to the kingdom. But maybe you have other plans. If so, you may have to ask yourself if you are willing to step into God's will for your life and pray the prayer Jesus prayed in the Garden of Gethsemane: "Lord, not my will but yours." If you do, it's like you are telling God, "I chose to live the life I didn't choose, and I plan to live the life I didn't plan."[4]

Following the will of God will always result in unexpected miracles.

Here's a poem I wrote that helps explain God's training process when it comes to seeking (and finding) his will and miraculous answers:

Is it just me or have you seen the way God answers
prayer?
I asked for hope, and then I found he trained me
through despair.
But once I asked for courage, then faced an awesome
fear.
So then I asked that God himself would show me
he was near.
The more I asked the more I found that God heard
every plea—
For every time I asked for help he taught me to
believe.
Because of him the battle's won; his grace has set me
free.
I once was lost but now I'm found, was blind but
now I see.

In other words, we are all living out Proverbs 16:9, which explains, "A man's heart plans his way, but the LORD directs his steps" (NKJV).

Dear Lord,

I give you my dreams, hopes, and plans and ask for your presence to ignite them, but in doing so, I pray not my will or my way but yours. Direct my path and fill it with miracles of strength, wisdom, prosperity, courage, patience, love, and favor.

I thank you that I can overcome the flaming arrows of discouragement, depression, fear, and confusion from the enemy. I can overcome these attacks because of my weapons of warfare, which include my hope and faith in you, my salvation, your righteousness, your peace, and my prayers that I bring to you in the name of Jesus—the name above all names, the name to which every spiritual authority must submit.

Lord, I choose you. I choose to cling to the cord of hope that you have given me. Thank you that as I cling to it my burdens become lighter and my future becomes brighter. In Jesus's name, amen.

Max Lucado says, "Having a Savior in Christ means that the hopeless have hope, the dead have life, and the abandoned have Good News."[5]

> *"Having a Savior in Christ means that the hopeless have hope, the dead have life, and the abandoned have Good News."*

Behold Jesus

Hopeless would have described me. Thirty-eight years ago, when I was but a toddler, a Roman chariot raced through our village. My mother screamed for me to run, but my chubby legs could not compete with the hooves that bore down on me. I don't know if I tripped or if I was overtaken. All I know is that one of those beating hooves landed on the small of my back. My mother reached me in time to pull me out of the way of the crushing wheels of the chariot. But it was too late. I was already a cripple.

No matter what the doctors tried, my legs refused to work. My mother got into the habit of carrying me down to the pool by the Sheep Gate in our little town of Bethsaida. We all knew the stories that angels frequented that pool, and whenever they stirred the waters, the first person who splashed into them was miraculously cured.

My arms were strong enough that whenever the water rippled I would drag myself to the water's edge. But each time I discovered that the flutter of ringlets was caused by a breeze or that someone else had gone in before me.

Going to the pool for thirty-eight years had changed me. I no longer sat by the water's edge. Now, my aging mother would direct my young nephews to lean me against a column so that I could comfortably rest in its shade. At the end of the day, my mother, who had once been so eager, no longer asked, "Did the waters stir today?"

She knew what I knew. My situation was hopeless.

But one day a stranger came to the pool and gazed not so much on the still waters but on the pitiful souls who gathered around them: the blind, the lame, and the paralyzed. The stranger shielded his eyes and spotted me in the shade. "You, do you want to get well?" he asked me.

I could taste my bitterness. "Sir, I have no one to help me get to the water. Someone is always before me."

He studied me then, as if he knew that I had long ago quit trying to be the first into the pool. Then he commanded, "Get up! Pick up your mat and walk!"

At his words, hope and strength flooded my being. I reached for the corner of my mat as my knees began to bend with purpose—something I'd been unable to do for thirty-eight years. Then, as if powered by new energy, I felt my thin legs rise to support my body. I was standing! I took a step toward the stranger, wondering, *Who is this who commanded me to stand?*

The stranger smiled at my surprise, and my vision suddenly blurred. I wiped at my eyes with my sleeve and looked back to discover the stranger had vanished into the crowded street.

That day, my first baby steps turned into steady strides, which was big news in my town. It didn't take long for the religious leaders to sniff me out. "Who was this stranger who told you to pick up your mat and walk?" they demanded.

But I couldn't answer because I didn't know who he was, that is, until Jesus saw me in the temple. He said, "I see you are well. Stop sinning or something worse will happen to you."

How he knew my heart. I resolved from that moment that I would put my hope in him because once you behold the power of the Messiah, you want to be a better man (based on John 5:1–14).

Beholding Jesus in Prayer

Let's behold Jesus in prayer:

> *Dear Lord,*
>
> *I should never be surprised when you show up in the middle of my difficulties. It's as if you are asking me, "Are you in earnest? Do you really want what you ask for?"*
>
> *Yes, Lord, even if your answers to my problems don't come in ways I've imagined.*
>
> *And so it is that through you, and you alone, I can rise up and walk above my circumstance, I can be whole and sound.*
>
> *I choose you, I choose hope, and I choose to be whole in you. In Jesus's name, amen.*

Listening Prayer

When you are searching for hope, it's important that you learn to seek God's voice. The following exercise will help you do just that.

1. First, ask God to quiet your mind and to speak to you. Then read the following passages:

No one will be able to stand against you as long as you live. For I will be with you as I was with Moses. I will not fail you or abandon you. (Josh. 1:5 NLT)

God can do anything, you know—far more than you could ever imagine or guess or request in your wildest dreams! He does it not by pushing us around but by working within us, his Spirit deeply and gently within us.

> Glory to God in the church!
> Glory to God in the Messiah, in Jesus!
> Glory down all the generations!
> Glory through all millennia! Oh, yes! (Eph. 3:20–21
>   Message)

> And so, Lord, where do I put my hope?
>   My only hope is in you. (Ps. 39:7 NLT)

2. Next, read these verses again, slowly, and write down thoughts that occur to you. Then read them again, emphasizing different words or phrases. Then write down any more thoughts that occur to you.

_____

_____

_____

_____

_____

_____

_____

3. Read over what you have written to discern if God is speaking to you. You may hear from him right away,

or you may have to continue to practice this listening prayer as you continue to meditate on his Word.

Making It Personal

Dear Lord,

You are the only one in whom I can put my hope. How happy I am to know that you are with me for as long as I live. How delighted I am that no one and nothing can pull me from your presence—for you will never fail or abandon me.

I put my hope in you because you alone can answer my prayers, even beyond my wildest dreams. You work inside my heart and gently lead me.

I give you glory and praise! I praise you, the God of your church. I praise you, Jesus the Messiah. I praise you because your glory transcends throughout the generations and forever and ever. In Jesus's name, amen.

5

Experience Trusting in God

As for God, His way is perfect. The Word of the Lord has stood the test. He is a covering for all who go to Him for a safe place.

Psalm 18:30 NLV

In an upcoming chapter, I talk about my disappointment over losing a prayer battle. But after I wrote that chapter, God used that very disappointment to become the cornerstone of the miracle I was seeking.

Isn't that so like God? He gives us miraculous results despite what seems like a lost battle.

So what happened?

My friend Sue and I had been praying for her son "Jess," who had, years earlier, been sentenced as an adult for a crime he didn't commit—all because of a plea bargain made by another young man. Jess was given a harsh sentence despite the lack of evidence and the fact that Jess was a minor at the time. After eight difficult years of injustice, Sue and I were praying hard, battling hell itself as we appealed to the Almighty for Jess to be set free. But because of a mix-up in Jess's paperwork, not only was he denied parole, but he was also suddenly sent to what many believe to be the worst prison in his state, a prison filled with extreme rules and conditions and where inmates curse and yell all hours of the day and night.

> *Isn't that so like God? He gives us miraculous results despite what seems like a lost battle.*

This young man was so upset by this turn of events that he told his mother that after years of waiting on God he had finally come to the end of his faith.

I have to admit it was difficult to understand how the results of our fervent prayers had taken such a turn, and Sue and I were devastated. But God, as it turned out, was giving us the miracle we'd been praying for, only not our way but his.

The prison Jess was sent to was centered around a so-called voluntary program that served its own brand of cruelty toward prisoners, cruelty that included subpar food, no exercise privileges, and a daily routine of chanting self-help platitudes for hours.

Jess, who had *not* volunteered for this program, stood up to the officials by refusing to leave his cell to attend the chanting sessions, despite their promises and threats. "What does it matter," he told them. "I've been lied to so many times by prison officials. Why should I believe anything you say? Just throw me in the hole where at least it will be quiet and I can finally get some sleep."

As it turned out, because so many prisoners had been sent to the hole for refusing to leave their cells, the state was now looking over the warden's shoulder. Because of his audience, the warden knew he couldn't make an example of a young man who had always proven to be a model prisoner. So the next thing Jess knew, the right strings were pulled and he was released to a halfway house, where he is now thriving with a new job and even has a new girlfriend who loves the Lord. His faith is now stronger than ever.

All of these things happened in only a few weeks after it appeared all was lost and that God had "failed" to answer our prayers.

Perhaps, like me, you find it difficult to trust God when things aren't going your way. So how do we change our attitude? Personally, I think it helps when we:

- realize we don't see things from God's perspective
- give God our situations, no matter what
- invite God's peace into our situations
- rest in God despite our difficulties

We Don't See Things from God's Perspective

What panics us does not panic God because he's got a higher perspective.

Back in my college days, the days before everyone carried cell phones, I went on a trip with a couple of vans full of young people to a conference in New Mexico. We'd had an uneventful journey, that is, until we drove through Dallas on our trip home.

> *What panics us does not panic God because he's got a higher perspective.*

That's when the traffic became so congested that we lost sight of our lead van.

Our eighteen-year-old driver went into a full-blown panic. Even though we had a trailer in tow, "Danny" hit the gas and began weaving in and out of the crowded lanes.

"Slow down!" the six of us begged from our seatbelt-less seats. But Danny refused, hitting speeds of over 100 miles per hour.

That's when I got on my hands and knees and crawled down the center aisle to Danny's side.

"Please—slow down," I begged him.

"But we're lost!" Danny argued, his eyes searching the traffic on the freeway ahead as he suddenly swung the van into another lane.

I countered, "Of course we're not lost. We're adults. We can find our way home ourselves."

When we follow God, we are not lost—even when we happen to be in the middle of the worst jam imaginable.

To my relief, Danny eased back on the gas pedal, and six hours later we pulled into our ministry's parking lot all safe and sound and, not surprisingly, the first van to arrive home.

Instead of panicking, hitting the gas, and weaving in and out of traffic, sometimes the best solution is to slow down and seek God. When we follow God, we are not lost—even when we happen to be in the middle of the worst jam imaginable. Not only does God have perfect timing, but he also knows the way through all our troubles. So take a deep breath and follow him, even when you feel stumped, stalled, or unhappy about the detour in your path. Because it's like what my friend Sue, Jess, and I learned: God can use *anything* to accomplish his purposes. The key is beholding God and remembering that he is telling us, "Do not fear; I will help you" (Isa. 41:13).

Dear Lord,

Thank you that I am not lost when I am following you. Thank you that I can trust you to get me through any jam. I will trust you because I know you love me and have a better perspective of my problems than I do. I know that your solutions are better than my solutions.

So I am calling on you to deliver me from my difficulties and am granting you permission to lead me. I'm trusting that you know the best way to my miracle breakthrough. In Jesus's name, amen.

Give God Our Situations

Let's take another look at Isaiah 41:13, which reads, "For I am the LORD your God who takes hold of your right hand and says to you, Do not fear; I will help you."

Whenever the Bible mentions the right hand, it's symbolically describing authority. So when we give God our right hand, we are not simply asking God to lead us; we are asking him to take authority over us. I believe that when God has authority over us, we also come under his protection, as Psalm 33:20 describes: "We wait in hope for the LORD; he is our help and our shield."

My dad was a loving father who would have gone to any length to protect his children. In fact, because of his love and protection, he not only shielded my brother and me from the ugliness of the world but also protected us from harm.

I'll never forget the evening my family pulled our car and pop-up camper onto a raised camper pad beside the lake at the Red Hills campground. It was dusk, so we hurried to set up camp so we could prepare for our wiener and marshmallow roast.

Our car and camper barely fit on the campsite's asphalt pad, which stood about three feet above the rest of our campsite, which sloped down to the lapping water of the lake. As dusk deepened into darkness, I hurried along the pad's narrow edge to get the hotdog buns out of our camper. That's when I noticed something extremely long and slithery moving at a high rate of speed directly toward my feet.

> *Our God loves and protects us the same way a good father loves and protects his children.*

The pad was too high for me to jump down into the inky blackness, so all I could do was scream and jump *up*. Somehow, on the way back down from my jump, my twelve-year-old elbows caught on the hood of the car, and I was able to hold my feet up as a long copperhead snake slithered beneath me.

It didn't slither for long, because at the sound of my screams, my dad appeared with his shovel. The snake's deadly fangs would never again get the chance to strike me or any other child who might stumble into that campsite.

Our God loves and protects us the same way a good father loves and protects his children. God is like my dad and is ready to do battle for us, his children, and to be our shield and protector.

I love how Acts 17:28 describes God's love for us: "It is in Him that we live and move and keep on living. Some of your own men have written, 'We are God's children'" (NLV).

If our God loves and cares for us like a good father loves and cares for his children, why shouldn't we submit to his authority so that we live and move in him? Why shouldn't we give our situations and battles to him? Let's pray about it.

Dear Lord,

I give you my troubles, my battles, as well as my fears and worries. I thank you that you are a good and loving father. I thank you that you not only have authority over me but also are my shield and my protector. You are ready and willing to fight my battles for me. I submit to you and your love and care as I give my situations and battles to you.

I praise your holy name. In Jesus's name, amen.

Invite God's Peace into Our Situations

I was recently on a radio show discussing how God can take any circumstance and flip it into a miracle when a caller asked, "You prayed and your daughter lived, but we prayed and our son died of cancer. Where's the miracle in that?"

"I am so sorry you lost your son," I said. "Was he a believer?"

"Oh yes," the gentleman answered.

"I know this might sound trite, but because your son knew God, your son is now with God. He *is* healed."

Please understand that although the promises of heaven are wonderful, I would never trivialize this gentleman's suffering and loss. But the good news is that God's peace is for all, even in loss.

When Laura, my then eighteen-month-old daughter, was in a terrible car crash, she literally returned from the dead after surviving a year-long coma. But even though she lived, she came back changed—paralyzed and with brain damage. I grieved because I'd lost the gifted child she'd been, and I had difficulty accepting her new reality. But through it all, God gave me his peace. And trust me, having God's peace is a miracle for which I am most grateful.

81

This miracle of peace can also be yours no matter what you are going through or what you've lost.

This miracle of peace can also be yours no matter what you are going through or what you've lost. If you call on God, he will give you his peace.

Dear Lord,
I call upon you to give me peace even in my difficulties and loss. I cancel the spirit of grief in the power and authority of the name and the blood of Jesus and ask you to give me your peace instead. Lord, teach me to abide in your peace, no matter what I am going through. In Jesus's name, amen.

Rest in God Despite Our Difficulties

The most wonderful thing about trusting God is that we get to rest in him. In fact, Jesus said in Matthew 11:28–30, "Come to me, all of you who are weary and carry heavy burdens, and I will give you rest. Take my yoke upon you. Let me teach you, because I am humble and gentle at heart, and you will find rest for your souls. For my yoke is easy to bear, and the burden I give you is light" (NLT).

Wouldn't you like to trade in your heavy burdens for lighter, heavenly burdens? You can, but the key is trusting God more—because the more you trust God, the more you rest in his presence, and the more you rest in his presence, the more your burdens, fears, and heartaches will vanish.

Back when I was a college student, I went out to dinner with a friend. Even though we had no credit cards or money in our pockets, we ordered delightful meals of fresh garden salads, mashed potatoes, thick slabs of roast beef, and heaps of buttery asparagus, with the finishing touch of huge slices of cherry pie with scoops of melting vanilla ice cream on top. When the meal was over, the two of us headed for the exit. But the cashier stopped us. "You haven't paid," she cried.

My friend turned. "I'm the owner's son," he said.

The cashier blinked. "So you are! Have a great evening, Mr. Tucker."

Our meal was provided for simply because Rick knew how to enjoy the benefits of being his father's son. He had no need to worry about paying his bill because he was resting in the knowledge that his father would provide.

As you begin to see God as your loving father, you will begin to notice his many provisions for you. You'll also see that you have an additional benefit. You can call out to God whenever you are facing trouble, as Psalm 46:1 says: "God is our refuge and strength, an ever-present help in trouble."

Look to Jesus, who is standing before you now. The more you behold Jesus, the more your worries will seem like a waste of time and energy.

> *The more you behold Jesus, the more your worries will seem like a waste of time and energy.*

The best way to keep your focus is through reflection, study, Bible reading, prayer, and listening for his voice. Then you will feel as King David felt when he wrote Psalm 46:2–3: "Therefore we will not fear, though the earth give way and the mountains fall into the heart of the sea, though its waters roar and foam and the mountains quake with their surging."

When we behold Jesus, even our fears will disappear, and we can rest in him.

Behold Jesus

Timothy had been excited when his mother had given him permission to tag along with Jesus and his disciples, that is, as long as he promised to give her as well as his grandmother a full report on all Jesus did and said. His mother had even packed him a lunch of five small loaves of bread and two fish. "Be polite and try not to get in the Master's way," she'd told him.

But soon he stood at the edge of the Sea of Galilee, squinting at Jesus's boat as it disappeared into a shimmer on the blue horizon.

Nearby, a disappointed woman explained to her husband, "Jesus got word that King Herod beheaded his cousin, so he and his men have left by boat for some secluded spot to rest."

Her husband responded, "My cousin told me where the Master goes when he retreats from the crowds, and it's only a couple of hours by foot. If we hurry, we can be there when he lands."

Timothy followed the couple's lead as they set out to walk around the lake. Their little band of travelers quickly grew because as they passed the shoreside villages the people would call to them, "Where are you going?"

Timothy would call back, "We're going to see the Master!"

Soon the crowd grew into a throng of people, a throng that was waiting on the far shore when Jesus and his men landed their boat.

Timothy pressed through the crowd until the water lapped at his toes, the perfect spot to watch as Jesus and his men pulled their boat onto the beach.

"Jesus, help us," voices from the crowd called out. "We need your healing touch."

Peter rushed to Jesus's side. "Master, I thought you came here to rest."

Timothy saw the compassion in the eyes of Jesus, who said, "Never mind. My heart is moved toward these people, for they are like sheep without a shepherd." Jesus turned from Peter to the crowd and called out, "Bring me your sick."

Timothy was mesmerized as the lame limped forward, leaning heavily on their crutches. After a touch from Jesus, they let their crutches fall and ran back to their joyful families. But it wasn't just the lame whom Jesus healed. The blind could see and the deaf could hear.

In all the excitement of the healings, Timothy hadn't realized the lateness of the hour until the evening breeze kissed his sunburned cheeks and a crescent moon winked on the horizon. That's when he saw the concern on the disciples' faces. Timothy trailed behind Peter as he made his way to Jesus. Peter said, "Jesus, tell the people to go away to the nearby villages and farms and buy themselves some food, for there is nothing to eat here in this desolate spot, and it is getting late."

But Jesus replied, "You feed them."

Peter's eyebrows arched into deep wrinkles. "With what? It would take a fortune to buy food for this entire crowd!"

Jesus replied, "Go find out how much food we have."

As the disciples went into the crowd, Timothy followed, watching as the people shook their heads. One after another they said the same, "I dropped everything when I heard the Master would be here. I brought no provisions—nothing."

Finally, even though Timothy's stomach growled with hunger, he pulled on Peter's sleeve. Peter scowled down at him. "Boy, can't you see I'm on an important mission?"

Timothy held up his lunch sack. "I have food," he said simply, giving everything he had for the Master.

Peter looked into the cloth bag, then, with Timothy following him, carried the bag back to Jesus. Peter said, "Master, all we have is five loaves of bread and two fish."

Jesus smiled at Timothy, then told the crowd to sit down. Soon the five thousand men and their families were sitting in groups. Holding Timothy's lunch above his head, Jesus looked to heaven and blessed it. After the blessing, he broke the loaves and fish into pieces and gave some to each disciple. The disciples, in turn, also broke the bread and fish and passed the food through the crowd. Timothy watched carefully. No matter how many times the disciples broke the bread and fish, it was as if his original lunch remained.

Peter smiled down at him. "Here, son," he said as he broke off a hunk of bread and tore off a large piece of fish and handed Timothy the food. Then Timothy sat down with the crowd and ate his mother's rich brown bread and seasoned fish until he could eat no more. Afterward, he watched in amazement as the disciples gathered the leftovers into twelve baskets. How had the little he had given provided for so many, with so much left over?

The truth couldn't escape him. It was the Master! His touch, his presence was more than enough. Jesus could not only heal but also provide (based on John 6: 1–14).

Beholding Jesus in Prayer

We serve a God who saves us so that we can walk with him, a God who can heal and provide. Let's pray a prayer of thanksgiving and trust.

> *Dear Lord,*
> *Just as you had compassion on the crowd of hurting people, you also have compassion on me. I know you hear my voice when I call, "Help me, heal me, be my provider."*
> *It's amazing that you care for me, and it's also amazing that I can give you my worries and needs in exchange*

for your rest. I praise you for being my provider, and I thank you for all your provisions, even the provisions I've taken for granted. In your provision are abundance and care. I see that you are moving on my behalf even now, and I thank you. In Jesus's name, amen.

Listening Prayer

Just think how our lives would change if we really trusted God through everything. All it takes to get to this point is a chance to behold him. There's not a better way to behold him than by meditating on his Word.

1. First, ask God to quiet your mind and to speak to you. Then read the following passages:

   > Give praise to the LORD, proclaim his name;
   >   make known among the nations what he has done.
   > Sing to him, sing praise to him;
   >   tell of all his wonderful acts.
   > Glory in his holy name;
   >   let the hearts of those who seek the LORD rejoice.
   > Look to the LORD and his strength;
   >   seek his face always. (Ps. 105:1–4)

   > I have told you these things, so that in me you may have peace. In this world you will have trouble. But take heart! I have overcome the world. (John 16:33)

   > Let all that I am wait quietly before God,
   >   for my hope is in him. (Ps. 62:5 NLT)

2. Next, read these verses again, slowly, and write down thoughts that occur to you. Then read them again, emphasizing different words or phrases. Then write down any more thoughts that occur to you.

_____

_____

_____

_____

_____

_____

_____

3. Read over what you have written to discern if God is speaking to you. You may hear from him right away, or you may have to continue to practice this listening prayer as you continue to meditate on his Word.

Making It Personal

Dear Lord,

Thank you, Lord, for all you've done for me. So many wonderful things! I give you glory, for holy is your name! Instead of looking to my strength, I look to yours. I seek to behold your face.

Of course, because this world is still my home, I will have troubles, but I am in you, and you have already overcome the troubles of this world.

In peace I wait quietly before you. My hope is in you, and you are more than enough. In Jesus's name, amen.

6

Experience Deliverance from Evil

Resist the devil, and he will flee from you.

James 4:7

Imagine you are standing inside a lion's cage as the beast lunges at you with flashing fangs. But you're not at all worried because you know just the thing to say that will stop the lion in its tracks. "I rebuke you, you big old cat!"

I think if it were me, I'd forgo the yelling and try leaping out of the cage before locking the door behind me.

I mention this because, as you may have noticed, believers love to "rebuke" the devil. "I rebuke you, you old lion, you."

But how is rebuking the devil supposed to stop his attacks? I think rebuking the devil is like putting a hand on a hip and saying, "Devil, I strongly disapprove of you. So there."

Consider that such a remark may only serve to make the devil angry, especially as he's known to be a prideful being.

Perhaps that's why the Bible doesn't teach us to "rebuke the enemy" but instead to "resist" him (James 4:7).

What are the best ways to resist the devil?

- walk in the light
- avoid temptation
- break the enemy's assignments
- break the lies
- stand against the enemy

Walk in the Light

Would you want to be trapped with a killer in a pitch-dark room? Of course not! But when we don't walk in God's light, it's as if we live in total disregard of the dangers that lurk in the darkness that surrounds us. But the good news is that you are safe in the light of God's presence. That's when you can see where the enemy lies in wait so you can easily avoid his traps. Take encouragement from 1 John 1:7, which says, "But if we walk in the light, as he is in the light, we have fellowship with one another, and the blood of Jesus, his Son, purifies us from all sin."

> *I think rebuking the devil is like putting a hand on a hip and saying, "Devil, I strongly disapprove of you. So there."*

If you are ready to walk in the light, pray this:

Dear Lord,

Help me move toward your light and to walk with you. Set me free of pride, judgment, anger, resentment, rejection, doubt, grief, sorrow, fright, fear, depression, sin, rebellion, addictions, and laziness—in my mind and soul and as well as in every cell of my body. Forgive me for entertaining or agreeing with any of these sins, lies, and conditions. I turn away from all these things and choose you, your presence, love, forgiveness, and grace.

I declare with joy that I am free! I am free from darkness and can walk in the light with you. You have healed my heart and forgiven my sins. In Jesus's name, amen.

In the prayer above, as you submitted yourself to God, know that the enemy fled (James 4:7). You can now walk in the light as God's love continues to transform you.

Avoid Temptation

Another way to resist the enemy is to avoid temptation. Avoiding temptation or not giving in to those things we either know is wrong or not God's direction for us, is not without struggles because we all fall short of God's best. But when we fall short, God does not set himself to swallow or crush us. His grace and the blood of Jesus are powerful enough to cover whatever our sin. However, as Charles Haddon Spurgeon, a preacher from the 1800s, said, "[We] should avoid temptation, seeking to walk so guardedly in the path of obedience, that we may never tempt the devil to tempt us."[1]

When we tempt the devil to tempt us, it's like we've left a ladder next to an open window with a sign that says, "Come on in."

When we tempt the devil to tempt us, it's like we've left a ladder next to an open window with a sign that says, "Come on in." As it says in Ephesians, "Therefore each of you must put off falsehood and speak truthfully to your neighbor, for we are all members of one body. 'In your anger do not sin': Do not let the sun go down while you are still angry, and do not give the devil a foothold" (4:25–27).

Break the Enemy's Assignments

Jesus taught us to ask for deliverance from evil, though as R. C. Sproul, a prominent theologian, once said, "The original text does not say 'deliver us from evil.' If so, that would be 'evil' in the abstract sense and would require the use of the neuter gender, but the term 'evil' in the Lord's prayer appears in the masculine gender, so it's proper translation is actually this: 'Lead us not into temptation but deliver us from *tou ponērou* [from the evil one].'"[2] This means that Jesus himself wants us to ask for deliverance from "the evil one."

When you keep the name of Jesus upon your lips, you can swing your powerfully supernatural weapon of prayer.

Do we have the right to pray for deliverance? Yes, because Jesus has authority over Satan (Eph. 1:19–23), and Satan trembles because the presence of God is in us and with us. This means that through Christ we have the power not merely to "rebuke" the evil one but to call upon the name of Jesus to cancel the evil one's strongholds and assignments against us and our loved ones. In fact, 2 Corinthians 10:4 says, "The weapons we fight with are not the weapons of the world. On the contrary, they have divine power to demolish strongholds."

It should also be noted that Jesus told his disciples, "And I have given you authority over all the power of the Enemy" (Luke 10:19 TLB).

When you keep the name of Jesus upon your lips, you can swing your powerfully supernatural weapon of prayer.

Dear Lord,

Thank you that I can pray to be delivered from the evil one. In fact, I now ask for that deliverance from the evil one and his schemes, not just for me but for my loved ones, in the power and authority of the name of Jesus.

Lord, I thank you that I can plead the blood of Jesus over myself and my loved ones, and I do so right now. I also pray that you will protect us, lead us, and guide us through anything we may face or any storm we may encounter. Thank you, Lord Jesus, that you are with us and that you are above all names. In Jesus's name, amen.

Break the Lies

Pastor Charles F. Stanley says, "We listen to Satan's lies rather than God's truth." Stanley adds, "The last thing that Satan wants is for you to be and do all that God has created you to be and to do."[3]

Think about it. If Satan can use a lie to knock you off your mission, steal your purpose, wipe out your joy, or lessen your witness, he can diminish your threat—which is why he never tires of trying to deceive God's people. In fact, Jesus described Satan as "a murderer from the beginning, not holding to the truth, for there is no truth in him. When he lies,

If Satan can use a lie to knock you off your mission, steal your purpose, wipe out your joy, or lessen your witness, he can diminish your threat—which is why he never tires of trying to deceive God's people.

he speaks his native language, for he is a liar and the father of lies" (John 8:44).

Because of Satan's plans to deceive you, you can probably bank on the fact that he's already introduced you to a few whoppers, such as, "God doesn't love you." "God can't use you, or forgive you, or even let his presence rest on you." "You're hopeless; you might as well give up."

You can become so familiar with the enemy's lies that you start to believe them. Enough is enough! I think it's time to get mad and to kick his lies out of your life.

Recently, my friends and I began to break the lies in our lives, ministries, and families, and amazing breakthroughs began to happen. One mom prayed this "break the lie" prayer over her college son, and hours later he reconciled with his father, explaining he was ready to get off drugs. Wow!

Another friend prayed it over a long and deep misunderstanding she'd had with her sister. Hours later, over lunch, the lie that had stood between them for twenty years suddenly vanished, and the two sisters reconciled. My friend's sister, without being prompted, even apologized for the misunderstanding between them. Amazing!

Then I felt what seemed like a silly urge to pray over a novel in a series I had written with my friend Eva called The Potluck Catering Club. I had no idea what, if anything, might happen.

I was stunned when two days later I received an email from a once very hostile book reviewer who two years earlier had posted a damaging review about one of our books, a book she freely admitted she hadn't even read. I was surprised to read one of the most heartfelt apologies I've ever received. The reviewer asked for my forgiveness and told me she'd removed all traces

> *You can become so familiar with the enemy's lies that you start to believe them.*

of her review from the internet. Her email came without any prompting from me.

If you're ready to be stunned by what can happen when you break the lies in your life, it's time to move into the authority you already have over the enemy.

Dear Lord,
  I break the following lies in my life:
  - *any lies I believe regarding my life, situations, health, work, family, friends, neighbors, church, or ministry*
  - *any lies I believe about you or my relationship with you*
  - *any lies my family believes about you or their relationship with you*
  - *any lies others believe about me, my life, situations, health, work, family, church, neighbors, or ministry*
  - *any lies I believe about others*

  Open my eyes, as well as the eyes of my friends, family, church members, neighbors, co-workers, and other acquaintances, with your truth, which will set us free.

I replace any and all lies with your truth, Lord. I pray this in the power and authority of the name and the blood of Jesus. I also plead for your presence, love, joy, and grace over these situations and relationships. In Jesus's name, amen.

Stand against the Enemy

When we've done all we can to defeat the enemy, we need to stand in position wearing our armor. Paul says in Ephesians 6:13, "So use every piece of God's armor to resist the enemy whenever he attacks, and when it is all over, you will still be standing" (TLB)

> *When we've done all we can to defeat the enemy, we need to stand in position wearing our armor.*

But to do this, you will need the strong belt of truth and the breastplate of God's approval. Wear shoes that are able to speed you on as you preach the Good News of peace with God. In every battle you will need faith as your shield to stop the fiery arrows aimed at you by Satan. And you will need the helmet of salvation and the sword of the Spirit—which is the Word of God.

Pray all the time. Ask God for anything in line with the Holy Spirit's wishes. Plead with him, reminding him of your needs, and keep praying earnestly for all Christians everywhere. (Eph. 6:14–18 TLB)

Let's take a look at these pieces of armor again before putting them on in prayer.

• truth: know the love of God is for you

- God's approval: remember you've got grace, meaning you are wearing the righteousness of Jesus
- the good news of peace: know you can rest in the peace of God because of the good news of Christ
- faith: believe God is with and for you
- salvation: know the blood of Jesus has covered your sin so you can walk with God

Who wouldn't want to wear armor like that? Let's try it on in prayer to see if it's a good fit.

Dear Lord,

Thank you that you've created an incredible suit of armor just for me. I put on the belt of your truth around my waist, knowing your love encircles me. I put on the breastplate of your approval over my heart, knowing you're protecting me with the righteousness of Christ. I stand on the good news of peace, knowing I can rest in the good news of Christ. I carry the shield of faith, believing you are with me and you will deflect all the flaming darts of the enemy. I proudly wear the helmet of salvation, knowing the blood of Jesus sets me free from sin and death. In Jesus's name, amen.

Behold Jesus

Whatever oppression of the enemy you may face is no match for Jesus, as one demon-possessed boy discovered.

Caleb's arms thrashed, and a pot of lentils landed upside down in the fire pit. He could hear lentils sizzle as well as the sound of his own voice wailing as if from a great distance. His mother joined his cry and turned to his father. "Samuel! Caleb's fallen in the fire!"

97

His father's strong arms pulled Caleb away from the flames that licked his kicking legs. Strong hands pushed him hard onto the dirt floor and held him tight until his thrashing stopped.

Caleb tried to catch his breath, but soon his screams turned into sobs. His mother pulled him into her arms and rocked him back and forth. "My baby, my poor baby," she cooed.

"How many times this week?" his father asked her.

His mother checked the burn on his leg before looking up. "Three times, I think—it's hard to keep count."

Later, as Caleb lay on his pallet, whimpering in pain, his mother covered his burn with an oily salve, then looked up at Caleb's father, simply stating, "Jesus is in town."

"Do you think he could help?" Caleb's father asked.

"It's said he's delivered others."

"I'll take Caleb to see him in the morning."

After breakfast, Caleb's father carried him in his arms until they came upon a band of men resting beneath a sycamore tree. "Is the Master here?" his father asked them.

"He's out for a walk up the mountain," one of the men answered, gesturing up a rocky trail. "Can we help?"

"Oh, please. It's my son. He's possessed by . . ."

Caleb heard nothing more except for the sound of his own screams. "Leave the boy alone!" a voice growled from within him. The disciples leapt to their feet and gathered around him, shouting, "We command you, unclean spirit, to come out of the boy!" But the voice inside of Caleb growled and shrieked.

Suddenly, the crowd parted as a man stepped toward him. "What's all the argument about?" Jesus asked.

His father answered, "Teacher, it's my son. He can't talk because he is possessed by a demon. And whenever the demon is in control of him, it dashes him to the ground and makes him foam at the mouth and grind his teeth and become rigid.

So I begged your disciples to cast out the demon, but they couldn't do it."

Caleb still thrashed as Jesus turned to his followers. "Oh, what tiny faith you have; how much longer must I be with you until you believe? How much longer must I be patient with you?" Jesus gestured at Caleb. "Bring the boy to me."

Caleb wanted to fall into Jesus's beckoning arms, but he was powerless against the force that controlled his body. So instead of turning to Jesus, he rolled in the dirt, saliva bubbling from his lips.

"How long has he been this way?" Jesus asked his father.

His dad replied, "Since he was very small. The demon often makes him fall into the fire or into water to kill him."

Caleb kicked as his father tried to hold on to him. His father pleaded above Caleb's shrieks, "Oh, have mercy on us and do something if you can."

"If I can?" Jesus asked. His words were so gentle that Caleb almost missed them. "Anything is possible if you have faith."

His father replied, "I do have faith. Oh, help me to have more!"

Jesus said, "O demon of deafness and dumbness, I command you to come out of this child and enter him no more!"

Darkness pushed itself into Caleb's mind as he screamed as though his very soul had been ripped from his body—then all went black. How long he lay in the dirt, he wasn't sure, but slowly, his senses returned, and he heard the murmuring of the gathered crowd. "He's dead."

Then Jesus took Caleb's hand and pulled him to his feet. Caleb looked around at the stunned faces before looking into the kindest eyes he'd ever seen. "Jesus," he stuttered, startled at the sound of his own voice. His dad threw his hands skyward and shouted, "Praise be to God," and wrapped Caleb in his arms, weeping into his hair.

To pray stronger prayers, we must
call on the mighty name of Jesus.
His is the name above every name
that causes the enemy to flee.

Caleb smiled as he absorbed his father's sobs. The Master had delivered him from the evil one and pushed back the darkness. Because of Jesus, Caleb was now free (based on Mark 9:16–28).

Later, Jesus's disciples asked Jesus why they had not been able to cast out the demon, and Jesus replied, "Cases like this require prayer" (Mark 9:29 TLB).

To pray stronger prayers, we must call on the mighty name of Jesus. His is the name above every name that causes the enemy to flee.

Beholding Jesus in Prayer

It's time to behold Jesus when (and especially when) we are oppressed by the enemy.

Dear Lord,

Thank you that even in the face of oppression from the enemy you show up wanting to help me. I know you are with me, so I turn my eyes from the enemy's destructive mission against me to you and your love, hope, and plans for me.

Lord, you are so beautiful, strong, powerful, and righteous, and you have already defeated the enemy, as well as sin and death, on the cross. I choose to walk in your light. So instead of asking if you can help me in my circumstances, I say, "I know you are able and will help." I ask that you defeat the enemy in my difficulties. I say to the enemy now, "I cancel your lies and assignments in my life and my situation. In fact, I cast you out of my situation and tell you to go, in the power and authority of the mighty name of Jesus."

> I behold you, Lord, and that makes all the difference.

Dear Lord, thank you for loving me so much that you hear my prayer. Thank you that you are moving on my behalf, replacing the tormentor's schemes with your mighty power and presence. I behold you, Lord, and that makes all the difference. In Jesus's name, amen.

Listening Prayer

Jesus, God's Son, has already defeated the enemy by dying a cruel death on the cross and rising from the dead. But the key to understanding his gift to us is to continue beholding him and focusing on his love for us.

1. First, ask God to quiet your mind and to speak to you. Then read Romans 8:37–39 (NKJV):

   Yet in all these things we are more than conquerors through Him who loved us. For I am persuaded that neither death nor life, nor angels nor principalities nor powers, nor things present nor things to come, nor height nor depth, nor any other created thing, shall be able to separate us from the love of God which is in Christ Jesus our Lord.

2. Next, read these verses again, slowly, and write down thoughts that occur to you. Then read them again,

emphasizing different words or phrases. Then write down any more thoughts that occur to you.

_____

_____

_____

_____

_____

_____

_____

3. Read over what you have written to discern if God is speaking to you. You may hear from him right away, or you may have to continue to practice this listening prayer as you continue to meditate on his Word.

Making It Personal

Dear Lord,

Let me count the things that can separate me from your love for me as nothing! Let me name all the powers and entities that can pull you away from me as none.

There's no demon in hell, no angel in heaven who could truly separate me from you. The lies of the enemy may come against me, causing me to doubt, but you and your love are greater than those lies. I continue to break those lies, Lord, in the power and authority of your name, and replace them with truth, the truth that I am truly loved and forgiven by you. In Jesus's name, amen.

7

Experience God's Healing Power

But he was pierced for our rebellion,
  crushed for our sins.
He was beaten so we could be whole.
  He was whipped so we could be healed.

Isaiah 53:5 NLT

When you read Isaiah 53, you can't help but notice that not only did Jesus die for our sins, but he also died so that we could be both healed and whole.

Yet, most of us know people who believed this to be true but did not see the miracles they prayed for. Some of these people even felt angry enough to leave the faith, wondering why they were excluded from God's promises. At the same time, others experienced these same promises to their fullest extent.

What does it all mean?

First, I want you to know that I have seen wonderful healings. In fact, just a few weeks ago, I led the women of AWSA (Advanced Writers and Speakers Association), a group of interdenominational Christian authors, into an hour-long prayer session in which we prayed for one another, our families, ministries, and publishers. Near the end of the hour, I had those who needed physical healing come forward. Then I led everyone else to encircle them and pray:

Not only did Jesus die for our sins, but he also died so that we could be both healed and whole.

Dear Lord,
We come to you on behalf of these dear friends. First, we break any workings of the enemy off of them in the power and authority of the name and blood of Jesus. We ask that you replace the enemy's work with your loving touch, your presence, your power, and your healing—in the power and authority of the name of Jesus. Amen.

When we broke for lunch, many of the women stayed and continued to pray for those who had requested healing prayer.

Later, one of our prayed-over authors approached me and held up her hands. "Look, Linda! I had osteoarthritis in my hands. This morning my hands were little more than claws. I couldn't put my necklace on, and my roommate had to help me with my buttons."

But now Trish opened and closed her hands, wiggling her fingers. She rotated her thumbs, backward and forward. "Do you see this? I haven't been able to do this motion in two years, even with hydrotherapy."

I realized my mouth was hanging open, so I said, "Wow!" then, "Thank you, Lord."

"I can type again," Trish gushed. "Now I can write more books for Jesus!"

While this is an exciting story, I remember a very different and difficult prayer experience. About a year or two after the car accident that put my daughter in a wheelchair, I heard that a well-known television evangelist and bestselling author who moved in the miraculous was coming to Denver, so I decided to take my daughter to see him. That night, though the convention hall was filled with thousands of people, my daughter and I somehow managed to snag a spot near the stage.

When the event started with lights, cameras, and action, the crowd cheered as the healer took the microphone. Then something unexpected happened. In an unrehearsed moment, a man sitting near me grabbed my daughter's wheelchair and with the cameras rolling carried my beautiful toddler onto the platform and plopped her at the feet of this famed gentleman. I too climbed onto the stage, not willing to let Laura out of my sight. The faith healer stared unblinking at my paralyzed, brain-damaged four-year-old, then at me, before turning to the awaiting crowd, which sat in awe, desperate to witness a miracle. This man turned back and placed his hand on top of my daughter's head and simply prayed. "Bless her, Lord."

That was it.

We were suddenly pushed aside, and the show continued as three glamorous women appeared from nowhere, practically crawling onto the platform. They gave the audience the show they'd come to see—the women shook, swooned when the healer blew on them, and testified they had been miraculously healed of unseen maladies.

But Laura? She went home unchanged.

I was disappointed and a bit disillusioned by all I had witnessed, but I still believed God had something more for my daughter. So later that night, just as I had every night, I tucked Laura into bed and placed my hand on her head and prayed, "Lord, please restore Laura's brain."

I never thought much about this prayer but was glad that Laura continued to thrive and enjoy her life, though she remained paralyzed. Then, some ten years later, when a neurologist put Laura's latest CAT scan onto the viewer in her office, I stood up. "I hate to interrupt," I said, "but that's not Laura's film."

"Yes, it is," the doctor replied. "See, it has her name on it, and there's her shunt."

"Yes, but 50 percent of my daughter's brain was destroyed in that accident. The child in this film has a mostly intact brain."

The doctor smiled sweetly. "Your daughter's brain regenerated."

I sat down hard. Then it hit me. Well, what had I expected? This is what I had been praying for the last ten years! God had answered my prayers and restored Laura's brain!

What a wonderful miracle indeed.

So what does this mean? It means God is God. He's not a paid performer in a circus, he's not a genie in a bottle, and he's certainly not our personal vending machine. He doesn't perform because we have power over him. God moves in the miraculous because he's God. He's mysterious, and he sees our reality from a different and higher perspective. He knows that if he answered all our prayers, just the way we prayed them, some of the miracles we requested would actually be harmful not only to us but also to those we love. Author Elmer Towns explains it this way: "Sometimes people pray for things they think are good, but actually there is harm in the answers they

God moves in the miraculous because he's God.

seek. God does not answer their prayers because he wants to protect them."[1]

What we can trust about God is this: He's holy, majestic, powerful, awesome, our Creator, our Savior, and, yes, even our Healer. Though he answers our prayers, his healings may not always come the way we expect or desire. Some people are healed on this side of heaven, while others are healed upon entering heaven after a long, grueling battle here on earth.

But though you may long for heaven, don't do anything to harm yourself in an effort to escape your life now, because God wants to teach us many lessons before that day we see him face-to-face, including trusting him through difficulty.

As for my daughter, she told me she spent time with Jesus following the car crash that put her in a year-long coma. It could be argued that it was only after she awoke from the coma that she experienced physical disabilities. But after spending a year with Jesus, Laura came back to us with a heavenly perspective and has never once complained regarding her paralyzed condition.

Yet, consider my friend Trish, who certainly did experience an awesome act of God—right here on earth! Though I'm sure everyone who received prayer that day got a touch from God, she was the only one who reported a miraculous healing. Those who were disappointed that they didn't "get their miracle" need to know this: God is *still* moving, and our

> *Some people are healed on this side of heaven, while others are healed upon entering heaven after a long, grueling battle here on earth.*

> *In some cases, the miracle may come later or may not look like what we asked for. But even so, the miracle will come and will have the power to change lives for eternity*

stories are *still* being written, because God's power is *still* in play. In some cases, the miracle may come later or may not look like what we asked for. But even so, the miracle will come and will have the power to change lives for eternity. In other words, a miracle can fall into one (or even both) of the following categories:

- healed (physical miracle)
- whole (spiritual miracle)

Physical Miracle

Can a prayer turn God's heart to heal a person physically? Yes, at least according to King Hezekiah, who was told by the prophet Isaiah that he should get his affairs in order as he would soon be dead. The king turned his face to the wall and earnestly prayed for God's healing, and God answered his prayer, granting him fifteen more years of life (Isa. 38:1–5).

I love knowing that prayer can change God's mind. But as we pray, we must remember that God is God, and even when he doesn't answer our prayers for physical healing the way we want, he is still moving on our behalf.

When author Beth Moore wrote about the physical healing of King Hezekiah, she said, "God cannot love us any more or any less than He does at this moment. He chooses to heal us or not heal us for His own reasons. All His decisions come from His love, but whether He chooses to heal us or take us home, His love remains constant."[2]

As for me, I've prayed many desperate prayers of a heartbroken mother on behalf of my daughter, asking God to let her walk again. But so far his answer has been no, and Laura has been wheelchair-bound for over twenty years. But miracles still happen in both Laura's life and my own. For one thing, despite my daughter's disabilities, God has given us deep and abiding joy, a very valuable miracle for my daughter, myself, and our family.

I will soon share a prayer you can pray for physical healing, but first, we must discuss how to pray. Our prayers have even more power when they are prayed in both:

- God's will
- the power and authority of the name of Jesus

When these two ingredients are active in our prayers, we can be sure that God has heard us. Our response then should be to praise God, even before he answers.

But how do we pray in God's will? Many people are praying that it be God's will for them to win the lottery. They reason, "Well, why not me?" They may even come up with a list of what they believe to be great reasons, which they've explained to the Lord a time or two. But consider why lotteries are so flush with cash. The sad truth is that many people spend the money they've set aside for groceries and rent for a chance to win, thinking God will honor their "faith" in a lottery miracle. How disappointed they must be when they find that the jackpot went to somebody else.

You can see from this example how easy it is to justify our will over God's will.

Let's take a moment to behold Jesus as he prayed in the hour before his arrest. "Father, if it is Your will, take this cup away from Me; nevertheless not My will, but Yours, be done" (Luke 22:42 NKJV). The Message translates this same prayer as, "Father, remove this cup from me. But please, not what I want. What do *you* want?"

Jesus prayed this because he wanted God's best to be completed, not only in his earthly life but also in our lives for all eternity.

If Jesus could pray, "Not what I want but what you want, Lord," then perhaps we should follow his lead and submit ourselves to God's will too—because we can trust that the will of God will result in the greatest miracle of the most eternal value.

But why do we need to pray in the power and authority of the name of Jesus? It's because Jesus is the only door for which we can even come to God. Through the work of Jesus, who paid the price for our sins through the blood he shed when he died on the cross for us, God sees us in the righteousness of Jesus—not in our personal lack of righteousness.

Not only that, but because when Jesus defeated sin and death on the cross, he shook up the dark powers of this world, making his name above their names and every name. The name of Jesus has so much power that even the demons will flee at the sound of it.

If Jesus could pray, "Not what I want but what you want, Lord," then perhaps we should follow his lead and submit ourselves to God's will too.

Let's stop and pray for a physical healing in the blessed name of Jesus.

> *Dear Lord,*
> *I know you came to save me from my sins, but I also know you are able to heal me. So I come to you with confidence, knowing that you love me and that you hear my prayer. Lord, therefore, I ask you to heal me of _____. I know you can. But I also ask that you heal me if this is what you want. I trust you to give the best answer and result possible for me as well as for my eternity and the eternities of the ones I love. In Jesus's name, amen.*

Spiritual Miracle

I would categorize my and my daughter's miracle of joy as a spiritual miracle. A spiritual miracle is a miracle of emotional or spiritual well-being or healing, and the good news is that this kind of miracle is always God's will for us. A spiritual miracle can include things such as getting right with God, being healed of bitterness, or experiencing the relief of God's forgiveness of our sin.

A spiritual miracle is a miracle of emotional or spiritual well-being or healing, and the good news is that this kind of miracle is always God's will for us.

Recently, I spoke on the phone with pastor and author Max Lucado as I was interviewing him about his wonderful book *Grace: More Than We Deserve, Greater Than We Imagine* for my blog *Finding God Daily*. In the course of the conversation, I asked him how someone could find the miracle of wholeness. He said, "I think that one of the underutilized disciplines of faith is confession. After thirty years as a pastor, I believe most people carry around unresolved guilt—a regret, a stumble, a failure—and they've never talked to God about it. Satan uses this guilt because the commodity of Satan is condemnation. Satan wakes up every day wanting to figure out a way to make us feel guilty. The Bible calls him the accuser, and his goal is to condemn us and to create within us a feeling of condemnation."

"So how do we apply the solution?" I asked.

"If we could learn to quickly confess, 'Lord, I'm sorry for what I did. I accept your grace,' then we would live in a state of confession, not in a state of guilt. To live in a state of receiving this forgiveness from God, all you have to say is, 'Lord, I'm sorry; please forgive me.' Then confess specifically what you did. 'I looked at a woman in the wrong way,' or 'I spoke out of turn.'"

Max explained, "On the days I really apply this, I find myself practicing dozens of confessions an hour. But it's not a sense in which I'm just beating myself up. It's a nonstop conversation that takes place in the back of my mind between God and me, and it's so liberating!"

"Then there's the issue of deep-seated bad choices," Max continued, "choices we made years ago that have never been dealt with. Many people need to go back and have a good talk with God about them—about the night in the backseat of a car, or the drugs, or the abortion—some of the major issues we've never really let God forgive."[3]

This is great advice from Lucado, and we will follow it with a prayer.

Dear Lord,

Thank you that it is your will for me to be happy in you, peaceful, forgiven, and free from worry, bitterness, and strife. I cancel the enemy's assignments off of me in any of these areas in the power and authority of the name and blood of Jesus.

I confess the things I've been harboring from my past in my spirit, my secret (or not-so-secret) sins of _____, my fears of _____, my worries of _____, my bitterness about _____, and my anger and battle with _____.

Forgive me, Lord, of my sins, and forgive me for not bringing you these problems sooner. I lay them down at your feet and ask you to give me the power to let go and the power to overcome. Give me the power to love and to trust you and to forgive even those who don't deserve it. Help me to forgive, just as you forgave me when I least deserved it.

I rejoice in you, for you have made me whole. You have filled me with peace, joy, love, trust, and forgiveness. I overcome in you and your strength, for the battle belongs to you.

Thank you! In Jesus's name, amen.

Behold Jesus

I recently read about a traveling evangelist who actually kicks people in the face with his spiked boots as a way of laying God's healing power on them. As this is not what Jesus did, I would advise you not to rush to join his healing line. Know that when Jesus healed the sick, he did so with love, a kind word, and a gentle touch. If anyone should know about the gentle, healing touch of Jesus, it was a woman I'll call Nissa.

Nissa had gone to the Capernaum marketplace to gather a few vegetables to serve with the fish that she and her daughter Mariam were frying for their dinner guests. But even as she bartered over the garlic, onions, and leeks, Nissa could feel her head throb.

She rubbed her temples. Life had been more difficult for her family since her son-in-law, Peter, had taken to following that rabbi Jesus, leaving his fishing boat idle more often than not. But Nissa tried not to complain because this business was really between Peter and her daughter Mariam.

Nissa handed over her precious coins in exchange for her purchase and turned to leave, almost colliding with a Roman centurion who was hurrying through the market.

Nissa watched as the centurion burst through a crowd, which soon parted, revealing Jesus and his men. The centurion approached Jesus and said, "Lord, my servant lies at home paralyzed, suffering terribly."

Jesus replied, "Shall I come and heal him?"

Nissa stood in the shadows, listening to the centurion reply, "Lord, I do not deserve to have you under my roof. But just say the word, and my servant will be healed."

Jesus turned to the gathering crowd and said, "I have not found anyone in Israel with such great faith."

Then Jesus said to the centurion, "Go! It will be done just as you believed it would."

Nissa was watching the centurion turn to leave when she met the eye of Peter. He quietly approached her. "How go the preparations?" he asked a bit anxiously.

"No need to be early," she answered. "The little ones have been trying Mariam and me all day."

Peter looked worried, perhaps noticing the shine that had dampened her brow. "Aren't you feeling well?"

"Just a headache. I'll be fine," she lied, trying to smile.

But by the time she arrived back at the house, she felt worse. Her daughter took one look at her, then touched her forehead. "You are burning hot, Mama. You have a fever."

"I'm all right to help you, Mariam," Nissa replied as her daughter led her to her pallet in the adjoining room.

"No, you're not. You must rest now. I can handle the meal."

Nissa's protests must have turned to sleep because the next thing she knew the evening crickets sang as Mariam scurried around the house to light the clay lamps. Nissa coughed just as her son-in-law entered the house with Jesus, his men just behind.

"Mother's not well," Mariam told Peter, as if to explain why dinner was behind schedule.

The house was small, and even from the next room Nissa could easily be seen by the men. She felt hot embarrassment blaze through her fever. But before she could hide by turning to face the wall, Jesus was by her side, kneeling beside her as she lay on her pallet. When Nissa looked into his eyes, she could see they were filled with love. And Nissa, like the faith-filled centurion in the marketplace, suddenly believed that Jesus would heal even her!

She watched as Jesus gently touched her tiny, wrinkled hand and smiled down at her. "Nissa! Arise, my sister. You are well."

When Jesus said these words, it was as if the light of heaven entered Nissa's very being. The throbbing in her head disappeared, her urge to cough ceased, and coolness swept into her cheeks.

She sat up, energized. "Thank you, Rabbi," she said. He lent his hand to help her up. Nissa stood and looked up at

Take a moment to behold Jesus. Even now, he has stretched out his hand to give you his gentle touch, a touch you can believe will make all the difference.

him and grinned. "Rabbi, now that you have helped me, I must help Mariam serve the dinner." She turned back to her regal self and took charge of the supper.

Later, when Nissa saw that all of their guests were served, she was pleased, glad that the task was done, and glad because she had never felt better in her life, all thanks to Jesus and his healing touch (based on Matt. 8:5–14).

Has the telling of Nissa's story helped you realize that Nissa's secret to her healing was that when she beheld Jesus, she believed he would heal her? Take a moment to behold Jesus. Even now, he has stretched out his hand to give you his gentle touch, a touch you can believe will make all the difference.

Beholding Jesus in Prayer

Let's behold Jesus as we pray:

Dear Lord,

As I enter into this prayer, I enter into a greater aware-ness of your presence, and in your presence, you see me with such love. I take a moment to bask in your presence, and I ask that your gentle touch will heal me so that I can better serve you—healed, whole, and forgiven. As

I behold you, I ask that you grant me the grace of your healing touch. Thank you! In Jesus's name, amen.

Listening Prayer

Now it's time to practice hearing God's voice regarding healing.

1. First, ask God to quiet your mind and to speak to you. Then read Psalm 103:1–5:

   > Praise the LORD, my soul;
   >   all my inmost being, praise his holy name.
   > Praise the LORD, my soul,
   >   and forget not all his benefits—
   > who forgives all your sins
   >   and heals all your diseases,
   > who redeems your life from the pit
   >   and crowns you with love and compassion,
   > who satisfies your desires with good things
   >   so that your youth is renewed like the eagle's.

2. Next, read these verses again, slowly, and write down thoughts that occur to you. Then read them again, emphasizing different words or phrases. Then write down any more thoughts that occur to you.

_____

_____

_____

_____

_____

3. Read over what you have written to discern if God is speaking to you. You may hear from him right away, or you may have to continue to practice this listening prayer as you continue to meditate on his Word.

Making It Personal

Dear Lord,

I bless you, Lord, the Creator, the lover of my soul. I bless your holy name! Thank you for creating me and for creating me to be in you. I ask that you be blessed in every way possible. Thank you that you hear my prayer. I believe you will do what you say, just as the Roman centurion believed you would do what you said.

Thank you for forgiving my sins, every one of them. Thank you for healing my diseases and for saving my life and redeeming me from hell. Thank you for crowning me with your love and mercy, a crown I will wear not only now but also when I spend eternity with you. Thank you for wrapping me in your goodness and the goodness of your blameless Son, Jesus, so that I can walk with you. How beautiful you are. Thank you that I am forever young in your presence and that you renew my strength like that of the eagle. In Jesus's name, amen.

8

Experience Praising God

Give unto the LORD the glory due to His name;
Worship the LORD in the beauty of holiness.

Psalm 29:2 NKJV

Open the window and listen to creation as it worships God. Do you hear the trees clap their hands as the breeze nods their branches? Can you tap your toes to the chirps of the crickets and frogs? Do you hear the chickadees add their melodies to the worship?

Pastor and author Lou Giglio has also realized these sounds of nature's worship, including the roar of the ocean and the beats of the rotation of the stars as they add their rhythms of praise to their Creator. The *Christian Post* reported that Giglio's mix of unedited sounds of whales as well as the sounds of spinning planets as recorded by highly advanced electromagnetic telescopes "sounded like a symphony." The *Christian Post* further reported that Giglio played sounds of this symphony at a worship event as he led the audience to sing Chris Tomlin's worship song "How Great Is Our God."[1]

How awesome. But before you think this is starting to sound New Age, note that Giglio's observations align with those of the psalmist, who said, "Praise Him, sun and moon; praise Him, all you stars of light!" (Ps. 148:3 NKJV).

> We ought not to claim creation's worship for ourselves but should instead join in to praise the Creator.

We've all observed nature praising God, but not everyone has clear insight into the purpose of the harmony. For instance, have you ever heard someone say, "When I'm in nature, I feel like I *am* God"?

We ought not to claim creation's worship for ourselves but should instead join in to praise the Creator.

Need a clearer picture? Check out Revelation 4:6–8, which says:

> In the center, around the throne, were four living creatures, and they were covered with eyes, in front and in back. The first living creature was like a lion, the second was like an ox, the third had a face like a man, the fourth was like a flying eagle. Each of the four living creatures had six wings and was covered with eyes all around, even under its wings. Day and night they never stop saying: "Holy, holy, holy is the Lord God Almighty, who was, and is, and is to come."

Adam Clarke's commentary explains that the creatures in this passage are "representatives of the whole creation."[2] So if the whole of creation is worshiping God, let's join in the worship:

- in spirit and in truth
- as a way to connect with God
- as a way to behold God

Dear Lord,

I join with creation's song of praise to you. I lift up my life, my heart, and my voice to praise you in spirit and in truth as I connect with you in deeper ways, behold your presence, and know you are near. In Jesus's name, amen.

Worship in Spirit and in Truth

When we neglect our worship of God, it's like putting an exquisite violin in a dark closet. That violin, no matter how grand its tone or design, becomes an instrument cut off from its very purpose. But when that violin is put into the hands of the maestro, it becomes an instrument that vibrates with magnificence and melody.

It's the same with us. We were created to worship God so that our lives can become a living melody of praise. But this can only happen when we worship God in spirit and in truth, a lesson Jesus taught the woman at the well. Jesus told her,

> *We were created to worship God so that our lives can become a living melody of praise.*

"Yet a time is coming and has now come when the true worshipers will worship the Father in spirit and truth, for they are the kind of worshipers the Father seeks. God is spirit, and his worshipers must worship in Spirit and in truth" (John 4:23–24).

But what did Jesus mean?

When Jesus mentioned "in spirit," he was referring to God's Holy Spirit, which rests on all who follow him. When Jesus mentioned "truth," he was referring to himself, for he later explained, "I am the way, the truth, and the life.

No one comes to the Father except through Me" (John 14:6 NKJV).

So to worship God both in spirit and in truth means we worship God through the spirit and truth of the person of Jesus. Compare this with how the people in Moses's day worshiped God.

Back when Moses led the Israelites out of Egypt, God's presence went before them in a cloud, a cloud that also rested in the tent of the holy of holies on the most holy relic of all—the ark of the covenant, a large wooden box covered with gold and filled with treasures:

- a jar containing manna from heaven: a sample of the heavenly bread God sent to feed his people in the desert
- the Ten Commandments: stone tablets of laws hand-carved by God
- the staff of Aaron: a staff that had belonged to Moses's brother, Aaron, and had once blossomed and even produced almonds

The poles that carry the ark are now our very own legs, and our bodies are his temple, where God's Holy Spirit rests.

The ark's lid was called the mercy seat and was carved with golden cherubim, winged creatures representing heaven's and creation's continual worship of God. The mercy seat was also the place where the high priest sprinkled the blood of a bullock to cover the sins of the people. Another interesting fact about the ark of the covenant was that it was too holy to be touched, and so when the people broke camp, it had to be carried with golden poles inserted into special loops.

Today, we no longer need the ark of the covenant to have a relationship with God because, figuratively speaking, the ark is now inside us. This is possible because when we trust in Jesus our hearts are sprinkled with his blood. Jesus is the:

- manna from heaven: the Bread of Life
- Ten Commandments: the fulfillment of God's law
- staff of Aaron: symbolic of the resurrection of Jesus

The poles that carry the ark are now our very own legs, and our bodies are his temple, where God's Holy Spirit rests.

This is absolutely amazing, and it means that the only way to worship God in spirit and in truth is through Jesus.

Dear Lord,

Thank you, Jesus, that I can worship you in spirit and in truth, for you represent the treasures of the mercy seat: the bread of life, the fulfillment of the law, and the resurrection. Because of you, my own body is the temple where God's Holy Spirit rests.

Thank you for your presence and for your intimacy with me. I thank you and praise your holy name. Amen.

Worship to Connect with God

Author Elmer Towns talks about the time when, alone in a Holiday Inn, he broke the gloom of a dreary morning by singing the Lord's Prayer. As he sang, he began to feel God's presence. He explains, "I have learned that when I worship God, He comes to receive my worship." Towns adds, "Jesus taught us that the Father seeks us to worship him. (See John 4:23.) So when I worship God in obedience to the Bible, God visits a Holiday Inn room to receive the worship I am pouring out to him."[3]

Towns makes a good point. Our worship becomes a touch point between God and us.

So when we feel particularly lonely for God because we're distressed or even under attack from the enemy, we can instantly open a direct channel to God through praise. Let's try out this truth by singing or reciting the Lord's prayer unto the Lord himself:

> Our Father which art in heaven, hallowed be thy
> name.
> Thy kingdom come, Thy will be done in earth, as it
> is in heaven.
> Give us this day our daily bread.
> And forgive us our debts, as we forgive our debtors.
> And lead us not into temptation, but deliver us from
> evil: For thine is the kingdom, and the power, and
> the glory, for ever. Amen. (Matt. 6:9–13 KJV)

Did you feel a connection? If you didn't, don't give up. Keep practicing praising God.

As you search for other ways to worship and connect with God, consider Rick Warren's definition of worship: "bringing pleasure to God."[4] The best way to bring pleasure to God is to live a lifestyle of worship, a lifestyle that helps you stay focused on God by continually praising him, as Hebrews

When we feel particularly lonely for God because we're distressed or even under attack from the enemy, we can instantly open a direct channel to God through praise.

13:15 declares: "Therefore by Him let us continually offer the sacrifice of praise to God, that is, the fruit of *our* lips, giving thanks to His name" (NKJV).

Paul's description of lifestyle worship goes beyond the praise of our lips, for as Paul explained in Romans 12:1–2:

> And so, dear brothers and sisters, I plead with you to give your bodies to God because of all he has done for you. Let them be a living and holy sacrifice—the kind he will find acceptable. This is truly the way to worship him. Don't copy the behavior and customs of this world, but let God transform you into a new person by changing the way you think. Then you will learn to know God's will for you, which is good and pleasing and perfect. (NLT)

When you are living a lifestyle of worship, it goes beyond music. It means you give of yourself, your time, and your resources as God leads you.

Little Eddie discovered the treasure of this truth during the Great Depression. Her dad had died five years before, and she, her mother, and her sisters had learned how to get by on very little. Then one Sunday morning the pastor announced that on Easter Sunday the church would take up a special offering for the poor family in their church. Eddie and her sisters were eager to help. They saved twenty dollars on their food budget by eating potatoes for an entire month. The girls made pot holders to sell to the neighbors and did odd jobs. By the end of the month, they had saved one ten dollar bill plus three crisp twenties. That Easter morning the girls didn't mind that they did not have new Easter dresses or had to walk in the rain to get to church. They felt rich. When they got to church, though still damp from the elements, they proudly put their offering into the plate to help the poor family. Later that afternoon, when their pastor dropped by their house, he gave their family the gift the church had taken up for the poor family: one ten dollar bill, three twenties, and seventeen ones.

The girls were shocked to discover they were the poor family. The next Sunday, despite their embarrassment of suddenly realizing their poverty, they went back to church and heard a missionary from Africa who was trying to raise money for a new roof for his mission. Their minister asked, "Can't we all sacrifice to help these poor people?"

The girls looked at each other and smiled, and their mother pulled the envelope out of her purse. The girls dropped it into the offering plate.

Later, after the offering was counted, the minister announced there was a little more than one hundred dollars in the plate. The missionary was so excited that he said, "I didn't know there was a rich family in this church."

The girls and their mother smiled at one another because they realized that the rich family the missionary spoke of was none other than their family.[5]

I love this true story from the life of Eddie Ogan, and I think it demonstrates a great truth. A sacrificial life lived for the Lord is not a life that has to be lived in poverty. Instead, it is a life lived in fullness and joy because it is a life filled with the presence of God.

A sacrificial life lived for the Lord is not a life that has to be lived in poverty. Instead, it is a life lived in fullness and joy because it is a life filled with the presence of God.

Dear Lord,

Help me to live my life as an act of worship, praising you and living my life as a living sacrifice. Help me to realize your presence, which leads to a life of riches and joy beyond imagination.

I worship you! In Jesus's name, amen.

Worship to Behold God

Worship is a way to open our eyes to God's presence.

I'm reminded of the time I was home alone reading a book when a deep male voice belted a shout from downstairs. "Jesus Christ is in the house!" In a heart-stopping moment, I thought I was about to see Jesus in bodily form walk up the stairs. That's when I realized some sort of power surge had kicked on my stereo, which had blasted out a rap by the worship artist Carmen. I will never forget how near God felt when the unexpected worship rang out from below.

God is always near and inhabits the praises of his people (Ps. 22:3). The more we praise him, the more we realize his presence is with us as well as in our situations. Then the more we know we are not alone.

> *God is always near and inhabits the praises of his people (Ps. 22:3).*

My friend, author, and speaker Thelma Wells learned this when she was a little girl. It seems her grandmother, "Mother Dot," kept her locked in a closet whenever her grandfather left for work. As Thelma recounts the story, she says, "Smell the closet with me. It reeked of tar and sweat, body odor, mildew, and mothballs. Being locked inside made me sick to my stomach."

Though the closet was a smelly, dark, and lonely place, Thelma recounts how as she sang songs like "What a Friend We Have in Jesus" and "Jesus Loves Me," her fear would lift and she would feel God's gentle presence. Today, Thelma has no trauma from her experiences in that dark closet because she knows God was with her during the abuse.

> *It's the song in our hearts that grants us the supernatural ability to know God is near.*

Thelma says, "Even when we are in the 'stinking closets of life,' we can trust Him to put a song in our hearts."[6]

It's the song in our hearts that grants us the supernatural ability to know God is near.

Sara Young wrote about this in *Jesus Calling*: "Fill up the spare moments of your life with praise and thanksgiving. This joyous discipline will help you live in the intimacy of my Presence."[7]

We can even thank God for the answers to our prayers before we receive them. In fact, when you are in prayer, instead of focusing on your concerns, which will keep you in a state of stress, try thanking God for his answers. Not only will you feel more positive, but you will also be reminded that God is moving and his presence is with you.

Behold Jesus

Rejected by our families, the ten of us lepers had no one to turn to except one another. If someone from outside our circle were even to touch us, they would be forever banned from worshiping in the temple. That didn't matter so much to me, a Samaritan, as I wasn't allowed inside to worship anyway. But it mattered to the rest of our band, all of whom had strict Jewish upbringings. Ironically, before we were all labeled lepers, none of the others would have even spoken to me on the street.

But that was then.

Now? My friends and I lived in a crude camp just outside our little village. We were close enough to town to catch a glimpse of our loved ones, but we stayed far enough away to ensure that they would never catch our terrible disease—a disease I wouldn't wish on my worst enemy.

Unholy apparitions of our former selves, we had no choice but to beg on the road, covering our faces and shouting out, "Unclean!" to keep others from getting too close. Sometimes kindhearted friends from our past would pitch coins into the dirt, coins we would gratefully gather with our stubby fingers. But generally most people hurried the other way, covering their faces with their robes, trying to ward off the stench of our rotting bodies.

Even our faces had been transformed into grotesque masks of pus and decay. We looked so pathetic that even if it wasn't against the law to touch us, no one in their right mind would even consider it.

We did what we could to stay alive and even kept a little vegetable garden in our camp. But it was hard to work the soil, considering we had lost all feeling in our hands and feet. Without pain to warn us, injuries would go unfelt, creating even worse problems, such as twisted feet, missing fingers and toes, and broken bones.

We were the cursed, at least according to Micah, who had been a Levite.

Last night, as the ten of us sat around our cooking fire trying not to singe our numb fingers, Micah told us the latest rumors about Jesus. "He's the one. I know it!"

"The Messiah? What makes you so sure?" I asked.

"Well, for starters, there are four kinds of healings the coming Messiah must perform, and two I've heard tell of, and another I saw for myself."

"What are these miracles?" young Sirus asked.

Micah's hoarse voice shook with excitement. "According to the Torah, he must heal the eyes of the blind, make the lame walk, and . . ."

Sirus interrupted, "The countryside is buzzing with tales of such healings by this rabbi."

Micah's laughter sounded like the croaking of a frog. "Yes, that's what I've been trying to tell . . ."

"But what about the healing you saw?" Sirus asked.

"It was a young boy with a mute spirit. Jesus healed him and set his tongue loose, even after his disciples couldn't."

"He healed a mute?" I asked. "Is that the third of the four miracles he must perform?"

Micah nodded, and I watched his face as the flickering light of our campfire caused the ooze of his ulcers to glisten.

Sirus asked, "So what's the fourth miracle?"

Micah pointed a bloody finger wrapped in an old strip of cloth into the air as he made his earth-shattering announcement. "The Messiah will heal the lepers."

Old Boaz, who had been silent until that moment, stared at Micah with his one good eye. "Is what you say true?"

"It's in the Scriptures. I read it myself when I studied in the temple."

My voice shook with hope. "So you really think this Jesus is the Messiah you Jews are looking for?"

"I do, and if he passes this way tomorrow, let's put him to the test and ask him to heal *us*."

"What do we have to lose?" old Boaz asked.

So we agreed. That night I slept fitfully, dreaming of my wife and children. How I longed to take them into my arms.

If only I could touch them, hold them, provide for them. I stared up at the stars as my salty tears dropped off my cheeks.

The next morning our little band got up before dawn and staked out a spot just off the road where Jesus would be sure to see us, even at the distance required by law.

The sun continued its climb into the morning sky, and then, suddenly, there he was. His eyes were gentle, though he walked as one with authority. The ten of us bowed and cried as loudly as our raspy voices would allow, "Jesus! Master! Have mercy on us!"

Jesus, who was leading his followers, signaled for his men to stop, and he called out to us, "Go to the Jewish priest and show him that you are healed."

My heart leapt within me. Only the Messiah would give such a bold order.

The next thing I knew, my friends were trying to keep up with me as I ran toward town to find the priest. As I ran, the bandages fell from my hands, and I saw they were clean from the ulcers and scales. I stretched out my fingers. They were no longer bloody or bent but straight, beautiful, and whole.

I pulled away the cloth that I used to cover my face and touched my cheeks. They were smooth like a baby's.

I stopped in my tracks, too stunned to continue my race. That's when I saw her, my own beautiful wife carrying a jar of water on her head as she hurried down the alley toward her mother's house. I called out to her, "Sari?"

When she turned and looked at me, she was so startled that she let out a small cry. I had to put out my hand to steady her jar so it wouldn't topple to the ground.

"Lucas! What's happened to you?" She looked into my eyes without fear. "You, you're clean? But how?"

My mouth went dry as I told her his name, the most wonderful name I knew. "It was Jesus the Messiah. He has given me back my life and . . ." but I couldn't say more, as the enormity of the gift Jesus had given me reduced me to sobs. I had to thank him!

"Jesus the who?" Sari asked. But I didn't answer because now I was running back to the one who had healed me.

When I found him, I fell at his feet. "Thank you, Lord, thank you!" I cried again and again.

He looked amused. "Weren't there ten of you?" he asked. "And here you are the only one not a Jew. Are you the only one who has returned to give me glory?"

I'm afraid I could do nothing but sob my gratitude. Jesus smiled down at me and said, "Stand up. Your faith has made you well."

And so I was. I ran back to town, running and leaping and praising God. When I found my wife, the two of us walked to the temple, where the priest pronounced me clean. I was able to return to my family and my life, ever so grateful to the Messiah (based on Luke 17:11–19).

Beholding Jesus in Prayer

Leprosy was a symbol of the curse of sin, a curse the leper himself could not remove. It took Jesus, the one who never sinned, to set the lepers free, just as the blood of our innocent Savior sets us free from sin and death.

So rejoice! Be like the one who ran back to praise Jesus.

Dear Lord Jesus,

I praise you that you were not afraid to touch me in my condition of sin. I praise you that your touch freed me from sin because you defeated my sin when you rose from the dead. Thank you for loving me so much that you endured the cross.

> *It took Jesus, the one who never*
> *sinned, to set the lepers free, just*
> *as the blood of our innocent Savior*
> *sets us free from sin and death.*

And now, I want to be one who falls at your feet and
worships you
> *I praise you! Amen.*

Listening Prayer

Let's continue in our time of praise.

1. First, ask God to quiet your mind and to speak to you.
   Then read Psalm 100:

   > Shout for joy to the LORD, all the earth.
   >> Worship the LORD with gladness;
   >> come before him with joyful songs.
   > Know that the LORD is God.
   >> It is he who made us, and we are his;
   >> we are his people, the sheep of his pasture.
   > Enter his gates with thanksgiving
   >> and his courts with praise;
   >> give thanks to him and praise his name.
   > For the LORD is good and his love endures forever;
   >> his faithfulness continues through all generations.

2. Next, read these verses again, slowly, and write down
   thoughts that occur to you. Then read them again, emphasizing different words or phrases. Then write down
   any more thoughts that occur to you.

_____

_____

_____

_____

_____

_____

_____

3. Read over what you have written to discern if God is speaking to you. You may hear from him right away, or you may have to continue to practice this listening prayer as you continue to meditate on his Word.

Making It Personal

Dear Lord,

Even the earth is praising you, and I join in, adding my own shouts of joy because you love me and set me free from the scourge of sin and death!

I worship you gladly with songs, because I know who you are—the Lord of all! I follow you like a sheep follows its shepherd into gates that open to provision and joy.

I give thanks to you, for your name will never disappear. I will worship you forevermore. In Jesus's name, amen.

9

Experience God's Love

I will always trust in God's unfailing love.
Psalm 52:8 NLT

I f you're like me, there are times you feel disappointed in
how you handle your challenges, frustrated that you aren't
further along in your life's goals or prayer life, or annoyed
that you've failed to love God, much less others, the way you
know you should. Perhaps you have flashes of insight of how
you could have handled a situation better than you did, and
you think, *What's wrong with me?*

We've all been there, and when we compare our failings
to our marvelous, holy God, we can't help but think, *How
could God love me? Doesn't he see who I really am?*

A couple months ago, I had a horrible day when everything
seemed to go wrong. Later that night, instead of going to bed,
I sat in my dark living room whining my faults to the Lord.
"Did you see me flare my temper instead of trusting you to
turn that situation to good? Lord, how can you tolerate me,

especially when I know better than to act that way? If I were you, I'd give up. I'd send a tornado to swallow me whole."

Suddenly, I recalled a day a couple years earlier when, while driving down the interstate, I actually ran my Ford Taurus completely through a half-mile-wide wedge tornado that had suddenly plopped down in front of me.[1]

God interrupted my thoughts with a gentle "gotcha" that warmed my heart. He said, "I did that once, remember?"

I couldn't help but grin as he spoke quietly into my spirit. "I was with you in that storm, and I got you safely through to the other side. Linda, you're not perfect, but I am. Because you exist in me, your sins are blotted out. I don't see your sins; I see you as forgiven."

I think we are all tempted to believe that because of our shortcomings God is more than a little annoyed with us. So like Adam and Eve in the Garden of Eden, we feel ashamed and naked—and so we hide from God. But God covered Adam's and Eve's shame with robes of fur created because he shed the blood of animals. Today, God covers our shame with robes of righteousness created because Jesus shed his blood for us. We are no longer naked before God but are clothed in righteousness. As Paul explained in Romans, "But God demonstrates his own love for us in this: While we were still sinners, Christ died for us" (5:8).

That was for my past sins, you may be thinking, *but what about my current or future sin?*

Because you are in Christ, you are wearing his righteousness despite your past, current, or future sin. I'm not suggesting this gives you the license to sin more abundantly. I'm suggesting that instead of making your sin your focus, you should focus on drawing nearer to God—because the nearer you are to him, the more his presence will transform you into the person he created you to be.

If you're still not sure as to whether or not God will forgive you of your sins, let me lead you in a little exercise. Think of three of your worst sins ever.

Did you think of lying or cheating? Then I have good news—God's grace covers both lying and cheating. Or maybe you thought of something more complicated like bulimia or cutting? Though those are painful activities and you may need help controlling them, believe it or not, God's grace covers them. Okay, let's think of really tough ones, like murder or abortion. God's grace is so abundant that it's big enough to cover those as

> *Because you are in Christ, you are wearing his righteousness despite your past, current or future sin.*

well. I didn't name the sin you were thinking about? No worries. God's grace covers that too. I'm not saying you won't face earthly consequences for your sins, but as far as God is concerned, when you are under the blood of Christ, you are forgiven no matter your crime.

That's amazing, as in amazing grace.

Let's stop and praise God that he shines his mercy on us:

Dear Lord,

You are so merciful to me. Thank you so much for covering all my sins with the blood, mercy, and grace of Jesus. I now lay my sins at the foot of the cross, and I thank you that they are not held against me but are instead forgiven.

Despite my past, present, or even future, you view me through the righteousness of Jesus. I am wearing his righteousness, not my own. Thank you! In Jesus's name, amen.

Myth Busting

I think there are three myths that keep us from drawing nearer to God.

1. I'm unloved and unforgiven.
2. God doesn't really care about me.
3. God can't love me when I'm angry.

Myth 1: I'm Unloved and Unforgiven

Though we've talked about God's forgiveness and the fact that he's not mad at us, the concept that we are forgiven is difficult to grasp. Consider this teaching story Jesus told about the prodigal son, a young man we'll call Sam.

Sam left his father's household and spent his inheritance on wine, women, and song. But when Sam's money ran out, his friends ran off. Before he knew it, Sam was so hungry that he ate pre-gnawed corncobs, leftovers from what he fed to a farmer's pigs.

Imagine Sam, sitting with those smelly pigs, thinking, *I've blown it so bad with my dad that I can never go home. Dad would never forgive me for all I've done.*

But one day he has a breakthrough in his thinking. He realizes, *Even my dad's servants are better off than me. I will go home and throw myself on his mercy, putting myself in his service as a slave.*

But when Sam's dad saw his younger son walking down the road toward home, he dropped everything and ran to embrace him. As Sam apologized, his father put a gold ring on his finger and new sandals on his feet to signify that Sam was not his slave but was in fact his cherished son (based on Luke 15:11–28).

God loves and forgives us even when we wander away. All

> *God loves and forgives us even when*
> *we wander away. All we have to*
> *do is turn around to embrace both*
> *God's presence and forgiveness.*

we have to do is turn around to embrace both God's presence and forgiveness.

Not long ago I had a dream. I dreamed God was sitting on his throne and spoke to me, saying, "I'm glad I am in your heart." I saw him reach down to place a tiny me in the palm of his hand before putting me in *his* heart. He told me, "I am in your heart, and you are in mine."

What a sweet dream. The more I think about it, the more I realize the truth behind it. Just as my children are in my heart, so I am in God's heart.

If we are in God's heart, what do we have to be afraid of? That's a good question, for Romans 8:38–39 says, "I am convinced that nothing can ever separate us from God's love which Christ Jesus our Lord shows us. We can't be separated by death or life, by angels or rulers, by anything in the present or anything in the future, by forces or powers in the world above or in the world below, or by anything else in creation" (GW).

> *Just as my children are in my heart, so I am in God's heart.*

It's time to officially bust the myth that we are unloved and unforgiven. We are in Christ, and therefore we are loved and forgiven by a God who fills our souls with his presence. Let's pray:

Dear Lord,

I thank you that I am both loved and forgiven by you. I thank you that nothing I did in my past or will do in my future can ever separate me from your love. You are in my heart just as I am in your heart. Thank you so much that even though there's nothing I can do to be good enough or to earn your love, it doesn't matter. You've given me the righteousness of your beloved Son to wear anyway. Because of this gift, you see me as beautiful, unblemished, clean, and forgiven.

I praise your holy name. In Jesus's name, amen.

Myth 2: God Doesn't Really Care about Me

Let's not forget the second son in Jesus's prodigal parable—the elder boy who stayed behind and helped his father till the fields and tend the flocks.

Imagine that after a hard day's work this son, whom we'll call Jeff, arrives home from his father's fields to discover his father has thrown Sam a party, despite the fact that Sam still smells like the pigs he just left. Jeff is outraged and refuses to enter the house. When his father comes outside to talk to him, this elder son complains, "All these years I've worked hard for you and never once refused to do a single thing you told me to, and in all that time you never gave me even one young goat for a feast with my friends. Yet when this son of yours comes back after spending your money on prostitutes, you celebrate by killing the finest calf we have on the place."

"Look, dear son," his father says to him, "you and I are very close, and everything I have is yours. But it is right to celebrate. For he is your brother. He was dead and has come back to life! He was lost and is found!" (based on Luke 15:25–32).

Let's reread a section of the father's speech, the part that says, "Everything I have is yours." In other words, the father is telling Jeff, "If you want a party, of course you can have one—for everything I have also belongs to you."

Let's bust the myth that God doesn't care about us. Perhaps you've been working so hard for God that you've forgotten to spend time with him. Stop and take some time to enjoy your own celebration with the Lord. Please pray:

Dear Lord,

I've been working so hard—tending to my job, church, and family—that I've forgotten to tend to our relationship. I'm tired of taking you for granted, thinking that you are celebrating everyone but me. Right now, right here, I'm taking this moment to enjoy you and to bask in your loving presence. I thank you that you are so close to me that your presence, your Holy Spirit, rests both in and on me. Thank you that everything you have is mine: love, joy, peace, faith, as well as provision to meet my every need. I bless your holy name. In Jesus's name, amen.

Myth 3: God Can't Love Me When I'm Angry

In the past six months, I had many wonderful answers to prayer, but as I mentioned in an earlier chapter, I lost some huge, heartwrenching prayer battles for loved ones. I felt numb, devastated, and even angry that so many things—so near to my heart—didn't turn out as I'd prayed. I felt so much pain that I wasn't sure I could write about God's love. Yet, God, in his wonderful grace, showed me I was in a perfect place to address his love, for I could better understand what so many are facing or feeling.

The first way God ministered to me after my "lost" prayer battles was to ask me, "Are you God? Do you think you know more about these situations than I do? Even though you don't

> *"Are you God? Do you think you know more about these situations than I do? Even though you don't understand why things turned out the way they did, can you not trust me enough to believe I am answering your prayers?"*

understand why things turned out the way they did, can you not trust me enough to believe I am answering your prayers?"

I was humbled, and though I still hurt from my losses, I turned to the Lord for comfort. Author John Townsend says, "When you are in a bad situation and don't know what to do, don't pull away from God. Draw closer! Love God in that situation. Invite him into your feelings, thoughts, actions, and reactions. Immerse yourself in his love, and you will find his way for you."[2]

Many others have survived difficulties and seemingly unanswered prayer this same way. Dr. Henry T. Blackaby's daughter Carrie was sixteen when she went through chemotherapy and radiation treatment for cancer. When Blackaby saw how his daughter suffered, he later wrote, "At times I went before the heavenly father, and I saw behind my daughter the cross of Jesus Christ. I said, 'Father, don't ever let me look at circumstances and question your love for me. Your love for me was settled on the cross. That has never changed and will never change for me.' Our love relationship sustained us through a very difficult time."[3]

Whatever you are going through, no matter what your circumstances, no matter how angry you've been at God, he understands how you feel, and his arm is not too short to save you (Num. 11:23). And though things may not be going in what appears to be the right direction, you can trade your anger for trust that God has everything under control. Everything really is going to be all right.

It's time to bust the myth that God can't love you when you're angry. Of course he can and does. But for your sake, it's time to let go of your expectations and say, as Jesus himself said on his way to the cross, "Not my will, but yours be done" (Luke 22:42). When you can pray in this way, you are trusting that God has a plan that will be the truest answer to your prayers. Let's pray:

Dear Lord,

Who am I to be angry at you? Please forgive me for my arrogance. But it seems to me that the prodigal son's brother and I have a lot in common. I often fail to see your love or presence in my offenses or difficulties. When your answers to my prayers are not as I'd hoped, help me to recognize your love and compassion toward me in my troubles, and give me faith to trust you anyway.

Even when I'm confused, bitter, and angry, I know you still love me. Your blood still covers my sins. And

---

Whatever you are going through, no matter what your circumstances, no matter how angry you've been at God, he understands how you feel, and his arm is not too short to save you (Num. 11:23).

---

then, when I allow you, you comfort me. You're a comfort to me even now. Help me to trust you more. In Jesus's name, amen.

The Love Exercise

As Max Lucado writes, "God loves you just the way you are, but He refuses to leave you that way. He wants you to be just like Jesus."[4]

Our transformation progresses when we begin to understand that God truly loves us. To help you more firmly grasp this understanding, choose to believe the following truths. Then read the corresponding Scripture passages and pray the prayers.

God Loves Me

The LORD your God is with you. He is a hero who saves you. He happily rejoices over you, renews you with his love, and celebrates over you with shouts of joy. (Zeph. 3:17 GW)

Dear Lord,
I choose to believe you love me! Nothing, no nothing, can separate me from your love because I am in Jesus Christ. Because of your love, you are my hero who saves me. I am so grateful that you rejoice over me, renew me, and celebrate me with shouts of joy.
I, in turn, celebrate you and declare my love and devotion to you. You are great and worthy to be praised!
Thank you! In Jesus's name, amen.

> Our transformation progresses when we begin to understand that God truly loves us.

God Forgives Me

Because of the sacrifice of the Messiah, his blood poured out on the altar of the Cross, we're a free people—free of penalties and punishments chalked up by all our misdeeds. And not just barely free, either. *Abundantly* free! (Eph. 1:7 Message)

Dear Lord,

I choose to believe that you have truly forgiven me and that I now wear Christ's robe of righteousness. Thank you that Jesus's blood washes away my every sin. Thank you that because of the work of Jesus you consider me holy enough to walk with you. I will no longer doubt you, for doubt keeps me from growing in you.

Thank you that my chains of doubt are broken and that I am now confident in you. In Jesus's name, amen.

I Am His Child

What marvelous love the Father has extended to us! Just look at it—we're called children of God! That's who we really are. But that's also why the world doesn't recognize us or take us seriously, because it has no idea who he is or what he's up to. (1 John 3:1 Message)

Dear Lord,

I choose to believe that I belong to you, and I choose to believe that I am your child. What a dear heavenly Father you are. You love me, provide for me, comfort me, heal me, forgive me, and abide with me, and just like with the prodigal son, you even throw me a party whenever I take the time to enjoy your presence. Thank you. In Jesus's name, amen.

Behold Jesus

After the sun began to sink behind the western hills, Peter hurried along with Jesus and the disciples to the upper room Judas had rented for the Passover celebration.

As they climbed the stairs, the hungry men breathed in the savory aroma of roasting lamb. Then they entered a large room that glowed with the light of oil lamps and candles.

Peter smiled. Everything seemed in order, and he joined the disciples as they settled at the low table that had been prepared for the feast. That's when Peter noticed there was no servant ready to wash their dusty feet. Had Judas forgotten to hire someone?

Peter felt relieved when a young boy carried a basin of water up the stairs. But to his horror, it was Jesus who laid aside his outer robe and wrapped a towel around his waist.

Before Peter could stop him, Jesus knelt before him and began to untie one of Peter's sandals.

Peter was horrified. "Lord, are you going to wash my feet?"

Jesus looked into his eyes. "You don't understand now what I am doing, but someday you will."

"No, you will never wash my feet!"

Jesus replied, "Unless I wash you, you won't belong to me."

Peter blinked and stared into the Master's earnest eyes. "Then wash my hands and head as well, Lord, not just my feet!" (based on John 13:1–9).

Jesus loved his disciples so much that he, God's only begotten Son, knelt before them to wash their feet because he came to serve them with his loving presence.

What should your response be to this revelation? Give Jesus permission to serve you, to wash your feet, as well as to wash away your sins, to heal your broken heart, and to embrace you with his love.

*Give Jesus permission to serve you, to
wash your feet, as well as to wash away
your sins, to heal your broken heart,
and to embrace you with his love.*

Beholding Jesus in Prayer

One night I experienced severe pain in my back and couldn't
sleep, so I tossed and turned for hours. Instead of popping a
pain pill or even asking God to heal my pain, I tried to behold
the Lord in my mind's eye. In that moment, I experienced
a sense of his presence, his glory, his love, and his awesome
power and majesty. And in that tiny glimpse of his essence, I
realized my pain was gone, my body had relaxed, and I was
drifting off to sleep.

It's time that we behold Jesus in prayer:

Dear Lord,

*I want to behold you. As I do so, I realize you are
shining your love over me. I receive your love. I repent
from saying I'm not good enough to receive the gifts you
want to give me. I accept them all because you love me
and want me to have them.*

*I, like Peter, now say to you, if you want to wash
my feet, you have my permission because I belong to
you. You also have my permission to wash all my sins
away, to heal my broken heart, and to embrace me with
your love.*

*In response to your love and gifts, I will serve you
with my love, do what you ask, go where you want, and*

remember that you are always with me. I know who I am. I am your beloved child. In Jesus's name, amen.

Listening Prayer

Let's dig a little deeper into the Word and prayer to see and experience God's love.

1. First, ask God to quiet your mind and to speak to you. Then read 1 John 4:7–12 (Message):

   My beloved friends, let us continue to love each other since love comes from God. Everyone who loves is born of God and experiences a relationship with God. The person who refuses to love doesn't know the first thing about God, because God *is* love—so you can't know him if you don't love. This is how God showed his love for us: God sent his only Son into the world so we might live through him. This is the kind of love we are talking about—not that we once upon a time loved God, but that he loved us and sent his Son as a sacrifice to clear away our sins and the damage they've done to our relationship with God.

   My dear, dear friends, if God loved us like this, we certainly ought to love each other. No one has seen God, ever. But if we love one another, God dwells deeply within us, and his love becomes complete in us—perfect love!

2. Next, read these verses again, slowly, and write down thoughts that occur to you. Then read them again, emphasizing different words or phrases. Then write down any more thoughts that occur to you.

_____

_____

_____

_____

_____

_____

_____

3. Read over what you have written to discern if God is speaking to you. You may hear from him right away, or you may have to continue to practice this listening prayer as you continue to meditate on his Word.

Making It Personal

Dear Lord,

You really love me! In turn, I love you, and in loving you, I give you permission to give me all of your good gifts. Because I love you, I also open my heart to love others, for that's the sign that I love you, that I love the people you put into my life. Please complete your perfect love in me as I love both you and others. In Jesus's name, amen.

10

Experience the Joy of the Lord

This is the day the LORD has made.
We will rejoice and be glad in it.
Psalm 118:24 NLT

I wish we could stay at the peak of our greatest moments: falling in love for the first time, the birth of our babies, or the day we got that all-important job. But life never sits still, and the next thing we know we're trudging through the valleys somewhere below our mountaintop highs. So how do we keep our mood up when our lives have either plateaued or gone downhill?

Lloyd John Ogilvie was once conversing with a man whom he described as a "moody" Christian. Lloyd told him, "Joy is no option; it's your responsibility."

That comment shocked the gentleman, who retorted, "You talk about joy as if it were a duty."

Ogilvie explained that he'd meant to say that. He later wrote, "In down moods, bad moods, bland moods, and moody times I've discovered that I can and must battle through my moods to joy."[1]

But is it really possible to change a bad mood into a joyful one? I believe that it is, though it can be a real battle, a battle I fought all week. The fact that I couldn't get a handle on my bad mood frustrated the smile right off my face. But what could I do? Every time I turned around I faced another serious disappointment or rejection. Soon my frustration turned into fretful sleeplessness, which then turned into fatigue. To top it off, I began to irritate myself because I spent too much time overanalyzing my disappointments instead of trusting God. Finally, I wised up and gave my disappointments as well as my nonstop fretting to the Lord in a prayer:

> *"Joy is no option; it's your responsibility."*

Dear Lord,

Please forgive me for entertaining my bad attitude, which I now tell to go in the name of Jesus. Lord, I give you my disappointments, fear, frustrations, and rejection because I'm tired of thinking about them and tired of trying to figure out how to respond to them. I choose to trust you even though my heart feels heavy. In fact, I give all my griefs to you now, and I apologize for not giving them to you sooner. I know you will turn all these things around and into miracles. What sweet relief!

Next, I choose joy, even though I don't feel joyful. I choose to praise you, even though I don't feel happy. You are great and worthy to be praised whether I feel happy or not.

Thank you for all your blessings, for all you've done for me, including turning my disappointments into joy.

Lord, I give you this day. Spend it with me as you order my steps. Thank you! In Jesus's name, amen.

After my prayer, a funny thing happened. Without even realizing it, my focus shifted from my disappointments to projects and people who required my attention. My mood was no longer sour because I'd finally quit thinking about myself and become mindful of the presence of God. Within hours the breakthroughs began.

First came a phone call that flipped one of the greatest disappointments of my week into good news. Then, while I was still on that call, the doorbell rang and the postman handed me the first copy of my new book, *When You Need a Miracle: How to Ask God for the Impossible*, a beautiful book filled with promise. Suddenly, the joy I had "chosen" was flowing through me in abundance, and so I stopped to pray, "Thank you, Lord. Thank you for everything!"

> *Sometimes your plans don't work out because God has better ones.*

The old adage proved true: Sometimes your plans don't work out because God has better ones. Stop struggling and surrender your plans, worries, disappointments, fears, and distress to God so you can give him room to move on your behalf.

Even if I hadn't received better news, I would have stayed committed to my battle to cling to joy, but not through my power but God's.

A Man of Joy

George Müller, an exceptional man who lived in the 1800s, was both an evangelist and the director of the Ashley Down orphanage in Bristol, England. Wikipedia says that Müller "cared for 10,024 orphans in his life. He was well-known for providing an education to the children under his care, to the point where he was accused of raising the poor above their natural station in life. He also established 117 schools which offered Christian education to over 120,000 children, many of them being orphans."[2]

And Müller did all this with a happy attitude. In fact, he had so much joy and faith in the Lord that he never sent out one plea for financial support, ever. With great joy, Müller knew God would supply his needs, and God did, every single time. What was Müller's secret to such faith? He once wrote, "I saw more clearly than ever that the first great and primary business to which I ought to attend every day was, to have my soul happy in the Lord. The first thing to be concerned about was not how much I might serve the Lord, how I might glorify the Lord, but how I might get my soul into a happy state, and how my inner man might be nourished."[3]

How did Müller get his soul happy so that he could both trust God and accomplish his daily to-do list in the right spirit? The answer is that he started his day meditating on God's Word, even before he spent time in prayer. He explained, "And thus my heart might be comforted, encouraged, warned, reproved, instructed; and . . . thus my heart might be brought into experimental communion with the Lord."[4]

Müller, who accomplished more than an army of men put together, did not make praying for hours, working into the wee hours of the morning, begging people for money so he could help orphans, or even fasting for days his number one priority. He instead gave that honor to seeking the happiness of his soul, which he found by meditating on God's Word. This goes along with Paul's challenge to us in Romans to "be transformed by the renewing of your mind" (12:2).

George Müller, who accomplished more than an army of men put together, did not make praying for hours, working into the wee hours of the morning, begging people for money so he could help orphans, or even fasting for days his number one priority. He instead gave that honor to seeking the happiness of his soul, which he found by meditating on God's Word.

This is such a good tip that we are going to practice meditating on the Word right now by focusing on several Scripture passages that speak about barriers to joy. Follow the instructions below for each of the four passages.

Meditating on God's Word

1. Read each verse. Then read it again slowly.
2. Read each verse once more, emphasizing different words and phrases as you read.
3. Rephrase each verse as a prayer to God.

   Fear—The apostle Paul once wrote the following words to Timothy to encourage him in his ministry:

   > For God has not given us a spirit of fear, but of power and of love and of a sound mind. (2 Tim. 1:7 NKJV)

Grief—Nehemiah, a man from 444 BC, had a vision. He wanted to rebuild the ruined walls of his beloved Jerusalem. He led an expedition that accomplished this feat in record time. Then when the men gathered to celebrate with a feast, they were struck with grief. Their hearts were broken because, though their walls had been rebuilt, the spiritual walls of their people were still in disrepair. So Nehemiah told the men this:

> This day is holy to our Lord. Do not grieve, for the joy of the Lord is your strength. (Neh. 8:10)

Anger—Many warnings and helps in the Bible deal with anger. The following verse also deals with fretting:

> Refrain from anger and turn from wrath;
> do not fret—it leads only to evil. (Ps. 37:8)

Bad attitudes—The best way to get rid of a bad attitude is by making the decision to rejoice, whether we feel like it or not.

> Rejoice in the Lord always. I will say it again: Rejoice! (Phil. 4:4)

As you can see, meditation is a great tool to help us maintain a happy soul before the Lord. Another great tool is when we learn to trust God on a deeper level.

Trusting God

Max Lucado once said, "Worry is to joy what a Hoover vacuum cleaner is to dirt: might as well attach your heart to a happiness-sucker and flip the switch."[5]

Worry steals our joy and takes our focus off of trusting God. But how do we maintain an attitude of trust? Let's take a lesson from David, who often wrote a kind of psalm known

> *"Worry is to joy what a Hoover vacuum cleaner is to dirt: might as well attach your heart to a happiness-sucker and flip the switch."*

as a lament. These laments have an interesting structure that includes:

1. a statement of the problem
2. a request for God to act
3. a decision to trust God
4. a breakthrough of praise

Let's take a closer look at David's lament in Psalm 13 to see this structure for ourselves.

A Statement of the Problem

> O LORD, how long will you forget me? Forever?
>   How long will you look the other way?
> How long must I struggle with anguish in my soul,
>   with sorrow in my heart every day?
>   How long will my enemy have the upper hand?
>   (vv. 1–2 NLT)

A Request for God to Act

> Turn and answer me, O LORD my God!
>   Restore the sparkle to my eyes, or I will die.
> Don't let my enemies gloat, saying, "We have defeated him!"
>   Don't let them rejoice at my downfall. (vv. 3–4 NLT)

A Decision to Trust God

> But I trust in your unfailing love. (v. 5 NLT)

A Breakthrough of Praise

> I will rejoice because you have rescued me.
> I will sing to the LORD
> because he is good to me. (vv. 5–6 NLT)

This is a great prayer outline to follow in which choosing to trust God in difficulties leads to praise. Try it now.

1. State your problem:

_____

_____

2. Request God to act:

_____

_____

3. Declare that you've decided to trust God in this matter:

_____

_____

4. Praise him:

_____

_____

_____

Banishing the Spirit of Trauma

Fear, grief, anger, and bad attitudes are negative emotions that can be caused by trauma. The spirit of trauma can sometimes slip into our lives through the open doors caused by disappointment, abandonment, illness, accidents, strife, rejection, crisis, and/or loss. Not only is this spirit of trauma assigned to steal our joy, but trauma, according to medical research, can also cause illness, which is all the more reason to bring this condition to the Lord in prayer. Psalm 34:17–18 says, "The righteous cry out, and the LORD hears them; he delivers them from all their troubles. The LORD is close to the brokenhearted and saves those who are crushed in spirit."

To rid yourself of the spirit of trauma, pray:

Dear Lord,

When I cry out to you, you hear me. You deliver me from all my troubles; you heal my broken heart and save me when my spirit is crushed. Therefore, in the mighty name of Jesus and in the power of his blood, I cancel any assignment of fear, generational curses, stress, or worry. I also cancel the physical effects of these spirits, including arthritis, cancer, digestive system troubles, disease, fibromyalgia, illness, pain, physical trauma from accidents, or other ordeals. Thank you for setting me free. In Jesus's name, amen.

Behold Jesus

How can beholding the Lord help you transform your sorrows into joy? Let's take a look at how this happened for a man named Cleopas and his companion, whom I refer to as Cleopas's cousin.

159

There was no reason to stay.

Only a few days before, the two cousins had tagged along with the disciples, their feet skipping on the shiny green carpet of freshly plucked palm branches. The crowd had waved these branches and placed them on the road as a welcome mat for Jesus as he had triumphantly entered Jerusalem, riding on a donkey.

But now, two dejected figures trudged down this dusty road back to their hometown of Emmaus. Cleopas broke their silence with a heavy sigh. "And we thought he was the Messiah."

"Who else but the Messiah could have opened the eyes of the blind?"

"Or raised the dead?"

"But it doesn't matter now. Jesus *is* dead."

A stranger quickened his step to join them. "You seem to be in a deep discussion. What are you so upset about?"

The cousins exchanged glances before Cleopas retorted, "You must be the only person in Jerusalem who hasn't heard about the terrible things that happened last week."

"What things?"

"The things that happened some three days ago—to Jesus."

Cleopas's cousin explained, "Jesus was a mighty teacher and a great prophet who did incredible miracles. Everyone loved him, that is, except for the chief priests and religious leaders. They had him arrested and saw to it that he was crucified by the Romans."

Cleopas shook his head. "We're stunned by Jesus's death because we'd believed he was the glorious Messiah who'd come to rescue Israel from the Roman rule. But now, to make things worse, some women from our group went to his tomb this morning. They reported that Jesus's body was missing and that some angels told them Jesus is alive! Some of our men ran out to see the tomb, and sure enough, Jesus's body was gone, but so were these *supposed* angels."

The cousin confessed, "Now we don't know what to think."

The stranger laughed softly then said, "How can you be so foolish? Is it so hard to believe what the prophets wrote in the Scriptures? Didn't they predict that the Messiah would have to suffer all these things before entering his time of glory? Didn't David say of the Messiah, 'Dogs have surrounded me; a band of evil men has encircled me, they have pierced my hands and my feet. I can count all my bones; people stare and gloat over me. They divide my garments among them and cast lots for my clothing?'"[6]

Cleopas, his eyes downcast, replied, "True, David did prophesy that. But for what purpose would God allow these things to happen to Jesus?"

The stranger answered again, "The prophet Isaiah said it plainly. 'Yet it was our grief he bore, our sorrows that weighed him down. And we thought his troubles were a punishment from God, for his own sins! But he was wounded and bruised for our sins. He was chastised that we might have peace; he was lashed—and we were healed! We are the ones who strayed away like sheep! We, who left God's paths to follow our own. Yet God laid on him the guilt and sins of every one of us!'"[7]

The cousins walked in silence, and the stranger continued to quote the familiar passage which they both knew by heart. "He was oppressed and he was afflicted, yet he never said a word. He was brought as a lamb to the slaughter; and as a sheep before her shearers is dumb, so he stood silent before the ones condemning him. From prison and trial they led him away to his death. But who among the people of that day realized it was their sins that he was dying for—that he was suffering their punishment? He was buried like a criminal in a rich man's grave; but he had done no wrong, and had never spoken an evil word."[8]

Cleopas shivered and pulled his cloak tight against a sudden late-afternoon breeze. "Then these things have happened just as Isaiah foretold."

The three men continued to talk as their shadows stretched before them.

Soon, they stood in front of Cleopas's house when the front door opened and his mother ran to greet them. "Thank God you are safely home!" She turned to both Cleopas's cousin and the stranger and gestured at her modest home. "Dinner is almost ready."

The stranger acted as if he would go on, but Cleopas insisted. "The hour is late. Stay here with us tonight. Besides, I want to finish our conversation."

"Yes," his cousin agreed. "These things you've told us are amazing. We would love to hear more of Isaiah's prophecies."

"Indeed," the stranger said, quoting Isaiah as they entered the house. "It was the Lord's good plan to bruise him and fill him with grief. But when his soul has been made an offering for sin, then he shall have a multitude of children, many heirs."[9]

The men sat down on the woven rug as Cleopas's mother served a small loaf of bread. Cleopas turned to the stranger. "Do us the honor of blessing and breaking the bread."

The stranger took the bread in his hands and blessed it and pulled it in two.

Cleopas stared at the stranger's wounded hands, then fell back with a shout, "Master, it's you!"

But Jesus didn't answer because he had simply vanished.

Cleopas's mother ran back into the room. "What's happened?"

"Jesus has risen!"

When you behold the risen Lord,
or notice that he's with you in the
darkest of circumstances, there's no
force in the universe that can stop
the joy that will flood your heart.

She looked around, searching for Jesus. "But from where?" Her son answered, "From death itself."

Cleopas's cousin shouted with joy, "Praise God! We have just broken bread with the risen Messiah! Jesus is alive!" (based on Luke 24:13–31).

Like Cleopas and his cousin, when you behold the risen Lord, or notice that he's with you in the darkest of circumstances, there's no force in the universe that can stop the joy that will flood your heart.

Stop and take a look. Jesus is standing with you right now. Rejoice!

Beholding Jesus in Prayer

To help you see Jesus the way Cleopas saw Jesus, pray this:

Dear Lord,
*   As you did with the men on the road to Emmaus, open my eyes so I can see you and recognize that you are with me now and in my circumstances, working all things for the good. Help me to understand that you are saying, "I am with you right now."*

As I behold you, let my heart be filled with joy. You have risen! Your presence in my life changes everything. Thank you! In Jesus's name, amen.

Listening Prayer

One of the best ways to behold Jesus is to experience his transforming power of peace.

1. First, ask God to quiet your mind and to speak to you. Then read Psalm 5:11–12:

   > But let all who take refuge in you be glad;
   >   let them ever sing for joy.
   > Spread your protection over them,
   >   that those who love your name may rejoice in you.
   > Surely, LORD, you bless the righteous;
   >   you surround them with your favor as with a
   >   shield.

2. Next, read these verses again, slowly, and write down thoughts that occur to you. Then read them again, emphasizing different words or phrases. Then write down any more thoughts that occur to you.

_____

_____

_____

_____

_____

_____

3. Read over what you have written to discern if God is speaking to you. You may hear from him right away, or you may have to continue to practice this listening prayer as you continue to meditate on his Word.

Making It Personal

Dear Lord,

I am glad that I have hidden myself in you, the safest place imaginable. Your presence as well as your protection fill my heart with joy, and I sing your praises. You are great and worthy to be praised!

Your protection is like wings that you spread over those who love you. Not only are you a blessing, but you also bless me. You place your favor on me like a shield, protecting me from the attacks and schemes of the evil one. With your favor on me, I can trade in my fear, grief, anger, and bad attitudes for your joy. I cancel the work of trauma in my life, and I choose joy. I choose to trust in you. In Jesus's name, amen.

11

Experience the Peace of God

The mind governed by the Spirit is life and peace.

Romans 8:6

It broke my Mom's heart when, after fifty-eight years of marriage, she had to place Dad in a nursing home because she could no longer manage his advancing care needs. One morning, when she was feeling especially alone, she opened her daily devotional and read Isaiah 41:10: "Don't be afraid, for I am with you. Don't be discouraged, for I am your God. I will strengthen you and help you. I will hold you up with my victorious right hand" (NLT).

"That Scripture really spoke to me," she later explained. She lifted her small, wrinkled hand to show she had given it to Jesus. "Jesus is holding my hand. I'm not alone."

This sweet revelation was tested when, one afternoon, she tripped over a rug on her back patio while feeding her ninety-one-pound golden retriever. After she spent two weeks in a rehab hospital recovering from a cracked pelvis, I was able to fly in to help her transition back to her home.

While I was there, I volunteered to take her dog to the veterinarian to get her shots. Mom told me, "Tell the vet that Maggie May needs a new home. I hate to do it, but I can no longer take care of her and she's been so lonely since Leroy's been gone."

Later, when I explained the situation to the vet's receptionist, she said, "I think I know just the person to call."

A few minutes later, an eighty-four-year-old woman who had recently lost her faithful golden retriever to cancer was sitting next to me and Maggie May in the vet's waiting room. Miss Ginny hugged Maggie May and then clapped her hands. "This is such an answer to prayer. I've been looking for a golden retriever to replace my Buddy." Her eyes glistened as she explained, "You have no idea what this means to me."

The next day, as the hour drew near for Miss Ginny to come over to the house to pick up Maggie May, my mother put her face in her hands. "I've lost my sweetheart to the nursing home, my daughter is about to get on an airplane to fly home, and now I'm losing my Maggie May."

I leaned in to hug her quaking shoulders. "You don't have to do it, Mom. When Miss Ginny gets here, I'll go outside and tell her you're not ready."

My mother shook her head. "I know this is the right decision. It's just that I so hate to give up my dog."

My heart ached for her, and I said, "This is one of those terrible life-changing transitions, and I'm so sorry."

When the knock came, my mother couldn't face saying good-bye to her dog and disappeared into her bedroom. After I helped Miss Ginny get Maggie May into the backseat of her car, I came back into the house to find Mom sitting at the kitchen table, still wiping away her tears. She held up her devotional and said, "Listen to this." She began to read, "The only thing you can grasp without damaging your soul is My hand. . . . The most persistent choice you face is whether to trust Me or to worry. You will never run out of things to worry about, but you can choose to trust Me no matter what. I am an ever-present help in trouble."[1]

When she finished reading, she bowed her head to pray. "I choose to trust you; I choose your peace, Jesus," she whispered.

"Are you okay?" I asked, knowing my brother was on the way to take me to the airport.

She smiled. "Jesus is holding my hand."

When my brother arrived, Mom's sweet smile had been restored, and she was able to tell me good-bye without tears. I knew I'd witnessed the supernatural power of God giving my mother his supernatural peace.

Perhaps you, like my mother, have found yourself in heartbreaking circumstances you didn't choose, and so you're wondering, *How can I find peace in these difficult times?*

Experiencing peace doesn't necessarily mean you are trouble-free, but you can experience peace in spite of your troubles. Despite what you are going through—the valley

---

Despite what you are going through—
the valley of the shadow of death,
chronic pain or illness, or simply a
hard day at the office—the best way
to have a calm heart is to choose
to hold on to the hand of Jesus.

---

of the shadow of death, chronic pain or illness, or simply a hard day at the office—the best way to have a calm heart is to choose to hold on to the hand of Jesus. He will never let go because he is our ever-present friend despite our:

- problems
- worries
- fears

Problems

Have you ever contemplated how much easier it would be to have peace if you didn't have any problems?

Jesus told his disciples, "I have told you all this so that you may have peace in me. Here on earth you will have many trials and sorrows. But take heart, because I have overcome the world" (John 16:33 NLT). James even went so far as to say, "Dear brothers and sisters, when troubles come your way, consider it an opportunity for great joy" (James 1:2 NLT).

But how does one find great joy in adversity? If you want real joy despite your problems, the first thing you're going to have to do is to quit rehearsing, replaying, or reciting your troubles to yourself or others. In other words, you'll have to stop whining. The more you whine, the more deeply you will

The more you whine, the more deeply you will experience stress. So instead of whining about your problems, why not try praying about them to God?

experience stress. So instead of whining about your problems, why not try praying about them to God?

> *Dear Lord,*
>
> *You are the one who wants to hear about my problems, including _____. In fact, you are so interested in my troubles that you want me to give them over to you. So right here, right now, I do just that. I've prayed this before, but I'll pray it as often as I need to. My problems are now your problems. In fact, I take this opportunity to trade my stress for a greater trust in you.*
>
> *Instead of constantly reviewing all my troubles, I've decided to stop focusing on my troubles so that I can focus on you. I acknowledge that you are with me in, as well as despite, my troubles. Please heal the turmoil and stress of my heart and mind and replace them with your peace and joy. I now tell the enemy, "Go! I cancel your assignment to torment me with turmoil and stress in the power and authority of the name of Jesus."*
>
> *Lord, I ask that you give me a greater understanding that you are indeed with me. Teach me how to abide in you. In Jesus's name, amen.*

Worries

We should resist the temptation to worry, but sometimes it's hard not to let our imaginations take over. I'm reminded of the time my friend Eva and I were set to ride the New York subway for a day of sightseeing. When Eva inserted her subway card into the automatic scanner, she was able to push through the gate. However, when I tried to follow her example, the gate refused to budge. By the time I found my way through the gate and down the stairs, the subway platform was empty. Eva had left without me.

This wouldn't have bothered me so much except that it was my first day in New York City, Eva was my designated guide, and I had no idea where she'd gone. To make matters worse, since Eva was now a passenger in the underground subway, it would be impossible for me to call or text her for who knew how long.

At first I felt panic and then extreme worry as I imagined what it would be like to spend the day trapped inside the New York subway.

A half hour later when Eva answered her phone, it felt like a fifty-pound weight had been lifted off my shoulders. She asked, "Where'd you go? I thought I saw you get in the subway car ahead of me, but as soon as the door clanged shut, I found I'd followed the wrong woman." Who knew when I'd selected jeans, a red turtleneck, and a black leather coat that morning that I would be wearing what would appear to be the standard New York City uniform? But how happy I was when Eva gave me the subway lines and stops for the Empire State Building, where she was waiting for me.

Whenever we feel we've lost our way, we should turn to God for instructions and ask him for help instead of putting all our energy into imagining the worst-case scenarios.

We can connect to God through prayer. In fact, Philippians 4:6–7 says, "Don't fret or worry. Instead of worrying, pray.

Whenever we feel we've lost our way, we should turn to God for instructions and ask him for help instead of putting all our energy into imagining the worst-case scenarios.

Let petitions and praises shape your worries into prayers, letting God know your concerns. Before you know it, a sense of God's wholeness, everything coming together for good, will come and settle you down. It's wonderful what happens when Christ displaces worry at the center of your life" (Message).

To help you overcome worry, please pray:

Dear Lord,

Sometimes I have no idea where I'm going, where you're leading me, or what I'm going to find when I get there. And sometimes, as I concentrate on all the what-ifs in my life, I forget you.

I know I'm not going into my future alone. You are going with me, and you have everything under control. Forgive me for spending my time worrying about what could happen instead of trusting you, for you make everything come together for good. Forgive me for doubting. In Jesus's name, amen.

Fears

I flew into Sioux Falls, South Dakota, one Friday to speak at a two-day conference. When I realized I'd left my power cord to my laptop at home, I asked the dear woman who'd picked me up at the airport to swing by the local electronics store so I could purchase another one. My new friend dropped me off at the front door, promising she would wait for me there. But when I came out of the store, she was nowhere to be found. I searched the parking lot, walking to and fro in the blazing sun, until I finally saw what looked to be her car. But when I swung open the door and hopped inside, the young man who sat in the driver's seat screamed bloody murder, right into his live cell phone.

"Wrong car—so sorry," I said, hopping out.

Moments later, I found my missing driver, who had parked out of sight just behind an oversized SUV. I was relieved to have found my friend, but even so, I will never forget the sheer terror in that young man's face as long as I live.

Perhaps you've felt that same terror when you've had to face situations that frightened you. It helps, when facing your fears, to keep King David's words in mind: "God *is* our refuge and strength, a very present help in trouble. Therefore we will not fear, even though the earth be removed, and though the mountains be carried into the midst of the sea; *though* its waters roar and be troubled, *though* the mountains shake with its swelling" (Ps. 46:1–3 NKJV).

You can't always control what enters your life, but you can count on God to be your refuge and strength. When you cry to him, he hears you. Let's cry to him now:

Dear Lord,

Thank you that no matter what's going on in my life you are with me. You comfort me, guide me, and take care of me. Give me your supernatural peace so that I will not fear, even when I face trouble or trials. Guide me through any problem that enters my life with the hope and the knowledge that you can produce miracles and new possibilities. I ask that you defeat the spirit of fear in my life and teach me how to better trust and enjoy your presence. In Jesus's name, amen.

Behold Jesus

Billy Graham once said, "Ask for God's peace and see what a transformation will take place in your life."[2] He went on to say, "Some of you believe you know Jesus Christ as your Savior, but you haven't really made him your Lord. You are missing the peace of God in your struggles and turmoils, and trials and pressures of life."[3]

But how do you make Jesus your Lord and find the peace Graham describes?

Once again, you have to behold him.

You can't always control what enters your life, but you can count on God to be your refuge and strength.

Saul was an A student of the Word and one of God's staunchest defenders, so much so that he worked to eradicate and imprison those Christ followers whom he deemed to be God offenders. Not only did he not believe the claims that Jesus had risen from the dead, but he also wanted to do everything he could to stop the spread of what he thought to be a vicious lie.

Once, he even guarded the robes of those who stoned the Christian named Stephen. Saul watched as a dying Stephen, his face glowing, gazed up at heaven to say, "Look, I see the heavens opened and the Son of Man standing in the place of honor at God's right hand!"

Saul's heart lurched. What an outrageous claim!

Stephen's death only enflamed Saul's determination to stop these Christians. He even requested and received special permission from the high priest to bring the Christians of Damascus back to Jerusalem in chains. But little did he know that he would soon have a face-to-face encounter with Jesus himself.

As Saul rode his donkey toward Damascus, he puzzled over the words Stephen cried before his last breath. "Lord, don't charge them with this sin!"

"The audacity of this heretic!" Saul muttered under his breath, his cheeks stinging with pride. Sin? Stephen was the sinner. His heresy, his allegiance to this Jesus, had gotten him what he deserved.

After hours of riding, and with Damascus now in sight, Saul kicked the sides of his donkey, trying to hurry his journey. But his donkey balked just as a bright light struck him like a bolt of lightning. Saul fell to the ground as a voice thundered, "Saul! Saul! Why are you persecuting me?"

"Who are you, Lord?" Saul asked.

The voice replied, "I am Jesus, the one you are persecuting!"

When Saul's men helped him to his feet, Saul had the physical manifestation of his true spiritual condition; he was as blind as a bat.

A few days later, Ananias, one of those very Christ followers whom Saul had come to arrest, prayed over Saul for his sight to return. Not only did the scales fall from Saul's eyes, but he could also see who Jesus really was: God's very own Son who had died for Saul's sin and the sins of the world (based on Acts 9:1–17).

Perhaps you still have a few scales over your eyes because you haven't come to terms with all of who Jesus is. Jesus is the one who came not only to set you free from sin and death but also to give you peace. But to gain it all, you have to give him everything—your sin, your worries, your fears, as well as your past, present, and future.

The revelation you may need to see concerning Jesus is this: He is trustworthy, and you can, like Saul, who became known as the apostle Paul, dedicate your life to following him as both your Savior and Lord.

Do you want peace? Behold, Jesus is standing before you now, removing the scales from your eyes. Fall at his feet and dedicate your life to him, regardless of the cost.

Behold, Jesus is standing before you now, removing the scales from your eyes. Fall at his feet and dedicate your life to him, regardless of the cost.

Beholding Jesus in Prayer

Dear Lord Jesus,

I want to behold you. Please take off any remaining scales from my eyes so I can see who you really are. When I think of you, I see you sitting in heaven on the right side of God. You are smiling back at me in love. I humbly bow at your nail-pierced feet and thank you for saving me from sin and death.

Now, I give you not only my sins but also my entire life. I give you my problems, worries, and fears in exchange for your peace that passes understanding. I praise your holy name! In Jesus's name, amen.

Listening Prayer

One of the best ways to behold Jesus is to experience his transforming power of peace.

1. First, ask God to quiet your mind and to speak to you. Then read the following passages:

> For I am the LORD, your God,
>   who takes hold of your right hand
> and says to you, Do not fear;
>   I will help you. (Isa. 41:13)

177

You will keep in perfect peace
those whose minds are steadfast,
    because they trust in you. (Isa. 26:3)

Be strong and courageous. Do not be afraid or terrified because of them, for the LORD your God goes with you; he will never leave you nor forsake you. (Deut. 31:6)

2. Next, read these verses again, slowly, and write down thoughts that occur to you. Then read them again, emphasizing different words or phrases. Then write down any more thoughts that occur to you.

_____

_____

_____

_____

_____

_____

_____

3. Read over what you have written to discern if God is speaking to you. You may hear from him right away, or you may have to continue to practice this listening prayer as you continue to meditate on his Word.

Making It Personal

Dear Lord,

What a privilege it is that you have asked to hold my hand. I offer it to you now, glad that you are my designated guide who will never leave me behind. I can relax, because you know the way I should go, and you are leading me there, step by step. Because you love me, I know I can put my trust in you. Help me to keep trusting you so I can fully know your perfect peace.

I give my fear to you: fear of people, the future, my present, and even my past. I ask that you replace my fear with trust and peace. I'm so happy that you are always with me, even now. I'm relieved to know that you will never leave me or forsake me. Thank you. In Jesus's name, amen.

12

Experience More of God

Come near to God and he will come near to you.

James 4:8

Have you ever needed to hear from God, like immediately? I'm thinking about the time my then four-year-old son, Jim, had the mumps. Poor little thing. There he stood in the kitchen in his little red pj's, rubbing his sleepy, blue eyes. I hugged him. "You go get into bed," I said as I turned to put the last of the dirty plates into the dishwasher. "Mommy will be right there to tuck you in and to say your prayers with you."

But moments later, when I walked into his bedroom, Jimmy's race car water bed was empty.

"Jimmy?" I called.

When he didn't answer, a quick search of the house put me into a sheer panic. It was a panic my husband soon joined as we explored every nook, closet, and cabinet in the house before running outside into the darkness as we called, "Jimmy! Jimmy! Where are you?"

Our cries were met with silence.

Had Jimmy wandered into the dark street? Had my darling, towheaded child been kidnapped? A million heart-stopping ideas taunted me as I continued my race to find him.

Finally, after twenty minutes of searching, my husband said, "I think it's time we called the police."

I dialed 911 and sobbed into the phone, "My four-year-old is missing! . . . He's sick with the mumps. . . . We've looked everywhere."

"I'm sending a squad car to your location," dispatch told me.

I hung up and closed my eyes. "Where is he, Lord?" I asked once again.

A still, small voice repeated a message I'd heard several times in the course of my search. *Go to Jimmy's room.*

The first time I'd heard this command I had run to Jimmy's room, thrown off the covers of his bed, and then peered into his closets and toy box. He wasn't there.

So now, with my chin to my chest, I walked back into his room and just stood there, letting my tears fall into the stillness that settled around me. That's when I heard God's still, small voice say, *Look again.*

"But where, Lord, where?" I asked, looking around the miniscule room.

That's when I noticed it, a tiny wrinkle on the fitted sheet near the footboard of the bed. Curious, I leaned over and touched the wrinkle, and my finger connected with warmth. I pulled the fitted sheet off the mattress, and there was my sleeping child. He had wedged himself face up—thank goodness—between the water mattress and the footboard and had somehow managed to pull the fitted sheet over himself, creating an almost undetectable hideout. He'd fallen into a deep sleep before he could surprise me with one of his famous,

"Boos!" He was sleeping so soundly that he never heard his dad and me calling to him.

But God heard my cries and continued to gently whisper Jimmy's location to my heart. I finally had my breakthrough when I was still enough to stop my search, follow God's lead, and then step toward what seemed to be an unlikely solution.

Can you imagine if the police had arrived before I had found my child? Chances are, Jim's trick would have also tricked them, kicking up a massive search for a child who was actually where he was supposed to be, in his own bed.

The steps of how I heard from God to find my son can also be applied to our prayer lives. Those steps include the following:

- be still
- listen
- obey

Dear Lord,

I want to behold you and to draw closer still. Teach me how to be still so that I can become more aware of your presence. Show me how to truly listen, then lead me to obey what I've heard. In Jesus's name, amen.

Let's take a careful look at these prayer actions that will not only help us hear from God but also draw us closer still.

Be Still

Psalm 46:10 instructs, "Be still, and know that I am God." Being still before the Lord consists of two basic actions:

1. being still in the knowledge of God's presence
2. waiting on God to move

As for being still before the Lord, author and speaker Ruth Graham explains:

> I have discovered that one of the best ways to be still and quiet before the Lord is to spend purposeful time meditating on Him. This is one way we can "practice" God's presence. I do not mean meditating in some New Age sense but rather quieting our minds and turning our thoughts to the Scriptures and to God's character. Fredrick Buechner once wrote, "To *meditate* is to open the mind to a single thought so completely that there is no room left for anything else." For us, "that single" thought is God.[1]

But waiting on the Lord is also important. For example, back in my college days, I was the evangelism chair of a large campus ministry at Lamar University. One day, my committee and I met to pray about how we could share Jesus with our campus, an idea that seemed impossible. We had a budget of about ten bucks, and even if we used our money to buy a few bundles of gospel tracts, we wouldn't have nearly enough. So the question was, how could we make a campus-wide impact?

"I have discovered that one of the best ways to be still and quiet before the Lord is to spend purposeful time meditating on Him."

After a time of earnest prayer, the group decided the answer to that question was to earnestly pray for a "miracle day." Our miracle day wasn't so much a plan as it was a date on the calendar. Basically, we circled a date and asked God to perform a miracle to reach the students on campus for him. In other words, our only plan, after our time of prayer, was to wait on God to see what he might come up with himself.

My team and I were both giddy and nervous about the adventure, and when the day came, we found it to be disappointingly uneventful, that is, until about 4 p.m., when Michael, one of the members of our committee, rushed into our student center shouting, "God did it! He gave us our miracle!"

We gathered around him. "What's happened?"

"The student government just voted to spend thousands of dollars to bring in a chart-topping recording artist to campus next month."

"How's that a miracle?" Jimmy, one of the students, asked.

"It's a miracle because this artist just became a born-again Christian! Basically, our student government has inadvertently booked a campus-wide Christian concert."

Do not be afraid to call on God for a "miracle day" of your own so you can learn to wait on him.

Whoooaaah!

Sure enough, a month later the entire campus turned out to watch this performer sing his chart toppers then to share his faith and call our campus to turn to Jesus.

Not only was God's plan a lot more exciting than anything my committee could have come up with, but it also fit our budget because it didn't cost us a thing. My committee and I attended that concert, in total awe of what God had done.

Do not be afraid to call on God for a "miracle day" of your own so you can learn to wait on him.

Dear Lord,
I want to be still before you, to recognize and acknowledge that your presence is in me, around me, and on me.

I now give you my request for my own miracle day regarding _____. I ask that you move in your own miraculous ways regarding _____. And I thank you ahead of time for what you are going to do as I wait on you. In Jesus's name, amen.

Listen

Do you have ears to hear God speak? Isaiah 55:3 says, "Come to me with your ears wide open. Listen, and you will find life. I will make an everlasting covenant with you. I will give you all the unfailing love I promised to David" (NLT).

> *God speaks to us every moment, just not always with words.*

Many people don't think God will speak to them, but the truth is God speaks to us every moment, just not always with words.

Have you ever seen the rays of the sun burst through a dark, gold-trimmed cloud, fanning the horizon with glory? Have you ever felt the caress of an evening breeze as the stars pop one by one onto a veil of velvet blue? Have you ever felt a raindrop splash your cheeks, then looked up to see crystal droplets falling out of a sheet of gray? It's all as Psalm 19:1–4 describes: "The heavens proclaim the glory of God. The skies display his craftsmanship. Day after day they continue to speak; night after night they make him known. They speak without a sound or word; their voice is never heard. Yet their message has gone throughout the earth, and their words to all the world." (NLT).

Nature praises the Creator, but the Creator also uses nature to send love notes back to us. In addition to these displays of love, God speaks to us through:

- God's Word
- his still, small voice
- visions
- worship
- dreams

God's Word

God's Word can speak, as Psalm 119:105 declares: "Your word is a lamp for my feet, a light on my path." In fact, A. W. Tozer challenged, "Come at once to the open Bible expecting it to speak to you. Do not come with the notion that it is a thing which you may push around at your convenience. It is more than a thing, it is a voice, a word, the very Word of the living God."[2]

> *God's Word will speak to us, because God's Holy Spirit will bring life to the Word as we read it.*

God's Word will speak to us, because God's Holy Spirit will bring life to the Word as we read it.

His Still, Small Voice

When the prophet Elijah needed to hear God's voice, he waited in the stillness until God spoke, not in the fire, the earthquake, or the wind but in a still, small voice (1 Kings 19: 11–12). It's the same voice that will speak to us when we learn to create silences and to ask questions such as, "Do you have something to say to me, Lord? I'm listening."

Don't forget to keep your safety net in force so you don't follow the wrong voices. For example, God will never insult you, call you names, or whisper words of discouragement.

God will never suggest you commit a crime, harm others, or go against his Ten Commandments. So if you ever hear a voice of hate or ridicule, suggestions of discouragement, or even thoughts of suicide, you need to know that you are not tuned into God but to the voice of the enemy. Happily, you can silence the enemy's voice with a simple command such as, "I break your assignment of lies in the power and authority of the name and the blood of Jesus. You must leave—without speaking one more word to me. In Jesus's name, amen."

Take comfort in John 10:27, which says, "My sheep listen to my voice; I know them, and they follow me" (NLT).

To practice hearing God's voice, you should continue to read the Word and discern what it is saying to you, just like you've practiced at the end of each chapter. As you read a passage, ask, "Lord, is there anything here you want to say to me today?" Then write down any impressions you feel are from God. This practice will help you learn how to recognize God's voice anytime, anywhere. Note that the more you practice, the easier you will be able to hear.

Then use the ABCs of communicating with God, which we discussed in chapter 2, and be still before the Lord, listening to see if he might speak to you.

Visions

When I was eighteen years old, though I was eighteen hundred miles away from home, I saw a vivid vision of my father falling off the back porch of our house. When I finally got to a phone, I learned that what I had seen in my mind's eye had actually happened. Dad had fallen when the concrete steps had broken in half when he'd hopped off a stepladder. (Though the fall was dramatic, he was okay and had only a few scrapes and bruises.)

That incident seemed to open the floodgate, and suddenly I began to see, hear, and emotionally feel disasters of many kinds before they happened—a shooting, a murder, and an oil refinery explosion.

This was new territory for me, and I was terribly troubled. So I went to my pastor to see if he could explain what this meant. He listened with wide eyes then told me, "I have no idea what this is or even what to tell you to do."

Confused and frightened, I told the Lord, "If these visions are from you, that's fine." But I told the enemy, "If these visions are from you, I'm putting you on notice because I commit to pray for the people in the visions."

Today, to my relief, I know that Acts 2:17 declares, "In the last days, God says, I will pour out my Spirit on all people. Your sons and daughters will prophesy, your young men will see visions, your old men will dream dreams." So when I receive visions, I keep my promise and get on my knees and pray. I've often been privileged to see God's miraculous results to these prayers.

Recently, God showed me that a series of tornadoes would sweep through Dallas, Texas. So I faithfully prayed that that there would be no loss of life. The next day, several tornadoes did sweep through Dallas, but despite the widespread damage in a highly populated area, not one person was killed. I believe God in his mercy answered my prayer.

If you receive a vision of a coming trouble, God may want to use you to beseech his mercy and protection in that trouble. Please get on your knees and join me in prayer.

I believe my visions are a call to prayer because God wants to invoke his mercy through my prayers. This also applies to you. If you receive a vision of a coming trouble, God may want to use you to beseech his mercy and protection in that trouble. Please get on your knees and join me in prayer.

Worship

I have to admit that I don't just see visions of disasters; I also see visions of glory, especially when I'm in a worship service. There I'll be, minding my own business, singing a worship song along with the congregation, when suddenly I hear his voice say, "Come up."

Then in the Spirit I see a vision of heaven. I've often seen the Lamb of God standing on the throne and surrounded by a crystal rainbow that is alive and pulsating in waves of living colors.

Glorious!

I can't explain the why of these visions, except for the fact that worship draws us nearer to God than we realize.

Dreams

When I put my head on my pillow, or in the moments I am waking, I love to turn my attention to the Lord. Recently, as I was drifting off to sleep, I asked the Lord about a dear eighty-seven-year-old friend who had recently died from cancer. Nancy had gone downhill fast, and one evening, three weeks after her diagnosis, she'd lifted her hands and said, "Take me, Lord Jesus." Later that night, she left this world. Her family found her the next morning with a sweet smile on her lips.

As I lay in my bed thinking about Nancy, I asked, "Lord, what was the moment of her passing like?"

Suddenly, whether it was a dream or vision, I'm not sure, but I saw Nancy as if her earthly life was the husk of a seed that opened as her soul burst forth into a new dimension of wondrous glory, glory that glowed brighter by the moment as she transcended from this life into an eternity with her precious Lord Jesus. Then I heard a voice say, "It's more glorious than you can imagine."

I shared my dream with Nancy's daughter Carole, who was deeply comforted, which is probably one of the reasons God gave me that dream.

Dreams can also serve as warnings. Author Jack Deere's wife had a dream that warned the couple to pray protection over their daughter. Jack says, "Pay attention to your dreams. God might use one to save you or your loved one from disaster. I wonder how much love and mercy we may have missed over the years because we dismissed a dream God sent to warn us. 'For God does speak—now one way, now another—though man may not perceive it. In a dream, in a vision of the night' (Job 33:14)."[3]

These ways to hear God's voice are inspiring, and I wanted to share them with you because I believe many of us hear God's voice more than we realize or will admit.

What prevents us from hearing God's voice?

1. We don't pay attention because we are not reading the Word or spending time in prayer.
2. We argue because we don't like what we are hearing. This happened to me last week when I picked up a pint of soup from the deli. I heard a still, small voice say, "Don't buy this. It will give you food poisoning." But because I'd missed lunch due to spending the day in the dental chair, I quietly argued, "But I need to eat." I put the pint of soup back on the shelf and picked up the one next to it. "I'll get this one instead." Unfortunately,

after eating that soup, I spent the next twelve hours with food poisoning just as God had warned me. I wish I'd paid better attention.

3. We doubt that we heard God. When you're worried about this, pray, "Lord, is that really you? If it is, please confirm this message. However, if this is not you but my own wishful thinking, my fears, or a message from the enemy, give me wisdom to know the difference. I break any message that's not from you, God, in the power and authority of the name and the blood of Jesus."

Dear Lord,

I come to you, asking that you would open my ears to hear your voice. You are my shepherd who calls to me. Teach me how to recognize your voice above all others. Keep me from deception and lies and focused on your truth so that I follow you and no one else. In Jesus's name, amen.

Obey

What good is it if we hear from God but ignore or disobey him? As I just shared, I still sometimes make this mistake, but how blessed I am when I follow through in obedience.

> *What good is it if we hear from God but ignore or disobey him?*

For example, every year my ministry throws a conference for Christian women authors and speakers just prior to the International Christian Retail Show (ICRS). It's a ton of work, most of which falls on me and Andy, my part-time assistant. But it takes not only hard work but also cold, hard cash. The cost of planning four banquets in luxury hotels is shocking, especially when the hotel adds a 30 percent gratuity and tax charge to my bill. It's not that I want to deny the hotel and banquet staff a fair wage; it's just that I'm prone to sticker shock.

So as I looked ahead to the next conference, I felt done. I told the Lord, "Orlando? I don't think I'll go."

That's when God's still, small voice spoke to my heart. *But what if I should come?*

I had to laugh. "Well, Lord, if you want to come, then I'll go with you."

Despite my parents being in and out of the hospital, my book deadline, my speaking engagements both in and out of the country, the fact that my conference chairs couldn't attend because of family emergencies, and the food cost was so high that the hotel cookies ran ninety dollars per dozen, I decided not to worry about it, and so I didn't. With God's help, the conference came together beautifully and ended up being our most successful to date. Despite the high banquet costs, God provided, and we had enough money to pay our bill in full. But more importantly, God came, and he mightily moved among our women.

What was my secret to being able to forge ahead despite all the obstacles before me? I had heard from God and knew he was coming to our event. I knew I didn't have to strive, plead with him to supply my lack, or fret over my to-do list. All I had to do was the next thing on my list, in his strength, then count on him for the rest.

Bestselling authors Henry and Richard Blackaby wrote:

> When you seek a word from God, it must be with an attitude that is primed to obey. God's opinion is not just one of your options. God is not interested in debating with you about your best course of action. He already knows what that is. If you only respond to God on your terms and in your timing, you are not prepared to hear from him.[4]

I like how James puts it:

Don't fool yourself into thinking that you are a listener when you are anything but, letting the Word go in one ear and out the other. *Act* on what you hear! Those who hear and don't act are like those who glance in the mirror, walk away, and two minutes later have no idea who they are, what they look like.

But whoever catches a glimpse of the revealed counsel of God—the free life!—even out of the corner of his eye, and sticks with it, is no distracted scatterbrain but a man or woman of action. That person will find delight and affirmation in the action. (James 1:22–25 Message)

Dear Lord,

What good is it to hear your voice then ignore it? Help me to humbly obey you with joy, for I know that when you tell me to go or do, you are going and doing with me. I can then relax, because the weight of our joint venture is not on me but on you. You'll be both my strength and supply. In Jesus's name, amen.

Behold Jesus

Peter had the privilege not only to behold Jesus but also to obey him. Let's listen to this creative telling of Peter's experience based on the Gospels.

When my brother Andrew told me, "We found him!" I knew whom he meant because John the Baptist had recently told those of us who counted ourselves as his disciples, "Someone is coming who is greater than me. Follow him."

The odd thing was that when Andrew brought me to see Jesus for the first time, it was as if we'd already met. Jesus told me, "You are Simon the son of John. You will be called Cephas, or Peter."

Later that afternoon, Andrew and I returned to my boat, and we fished away the night. We caught nothing, but the next morning, Jesus met us on the shore and asked if he could climb aboard. My boat gently bobbed just beyond the shallows while Jesus spent the next hour teaching the people who'd gathered along the shore to hear him.

When the crowds dispersed, Jesus told my brother and me, "Go out into the deep water and let down your nets for a catch."

I protested, "Teacher, we worked hard all night and caught nothing. But I'll do it if you say so."

Moments later, we let our nets down, and they quickly filled with fish, their fins glowing like the silver they would fetch at market.

The weight of the catch almost caused my boat to sink, but that was nothing compared to the weight of my sins. I fell at Jesus's feet. "Teacher, I'm not good enough to be in your company. Walk away and never come back."

But Jesus said, "Don't be afraid. Follow me, and I will help you become fishers of men."

My brother and I did follow Jesus. Over the next year or so, we had him to our homes, listened to him teach, and watched him heal the sick, the blind, the lame, and even the lepers. As we soon realized he was the promised Messiah, we secretly wondered when he'd make his move to lead a revolt against the Romans. That's why I kept my sword with me, so I'd be ready when the fight began.

But when that day of violence came in the Garden of Gethsemane, not only did Jesus not fight, but he also rebuked me for defending him, even healing the ear I'd lopped off the servant of the high priest. But the worst moment came when I denied him three times, swearing and telling those waiting outside his trial that I'd never even met him.

I was heartbroken by my betrayal and devastated when they nailed Jesus to the cross, where he hung until he was dead.

The disciples and I mourned in hidden rooms for three days, that is, until the women ran to tell us they had seen Jesus, alive, in the garden outside the tomb. I wouldn't have believed, but soon I saw him for myself. Jesus had risen from the dead, defeating the kingdom of sin and death!

After that, Jesus appeared to us disciples several times. But the third time he appeared to me I was back to my fishing.

I didn't realize it was Jesus on the shore, but when he called to us to cast our nets on the other side of the boat, we did. Soon our nets strained under the load of our catch. That's when I knew! I leapt into the waters and swam the hundred yards to meet him.

That morning, Jesus and I talked as fresh fish sizzled on the hot coals he had already prepared for us. When I finished eating, Jesus turned to me with such intensity and asked, "Simon, son of John, do you love me more than these?"

My heart lurched in my chest. I answered, "Yes, Lord, you know I love you."

He replied simply, "Feed my lambs."

Then he asked me again, "Simon, son of John, do you love me?"

Concerned now, I answered him straight away. "Yes, Lord, you know I love you."

He said, "Take care of my sheep."

Then a third time he asked me, "Simon, son of John, do you love me?"

I thought my heart would break because it was apparent he no longer trusted me because I had denied him just as he'd predicted. But I answered with all my strength. "Lord, you know everything. You know I love you."

Jesus said simply, "Feed my sheep."

Before I could respond, he gave me bad news. "When you were young, you put on your belt and went wherever you wanted to go. When you get old, you will put out your hands and someone else will put on your belt and take you away where you do not want to go."

Though I was shocked by his description of my fate, I was unwavering. I was now willing to die for my King. Jesus must have seen my resolve, for he smiled at me then and repeated those words he had spoken when he had first called me so long ago: "Follow me."

I spent my life doing just that. I loved and trusted him even if it meant my death, for not only was I forgiven, but I was also a new man.

Beholding Jesus in Prayer

What Jesus told Peter by the Sea of Galilee is also for us. If we love him, we will follow him and feed his sheep.

Dear Lord,

I behold you. I praise you that you know my name and have asked me to follow you. As I do, teach me how to love and trust you more as we go on adventures together to feed your sheep, sheep that include my family, my church, my neighbors, and my co-workers.

I will follow you even when you take me directions I would not have picked, even into the shadow of death. Help me to stay close and to continue to see you every day. In Jesus's name, amen.

Listening Prayer

1. First, ask God to quiet your mind and to speak to you. Then read the following passages:

   > When the Spirit of truth comes, he will guide you into all truth. He will not speak on his own but will tell you what he has heard. He will tell you about the future. He will bring me glory by telling you whatever he receives from me. (John 16:13–14 NLT)

   > So you have sorrow now, but I will see you again; then you will rejoice, and no one can rob you of that joy. At that time you won't need to ask me for anything. I tell you the truth, you will ask the Father directly, and he will grant your request because you use my name. You haven't done this before. Ask, using my name, and you will receive, and you will have abundant joy. (John 16:22–24 NLT)

   > I have told you all this so that you may have peace in me. Here on earth you will have many trials and sorrows. But take heart, because I have overcome the world. (John 16:33 NLT)

   > Jesus came and told his disciples, "I have been given all authority in heaven and on earth. Therefore, go and make disciples of all the nations, baptizing them in the name of the Father and the Son and the Holy Spirit. Teach these new disciples to obey all the commands I have given you. And be sure of this: I am with you always, even to the end of the age." (Matt. 28:18–20 NLT)

2. Next, read these verses again, slowly, and write down thoughts that occur to you. Then read them again, emphasizing different words or phrases. Then write down any more thoughts that occur to you.

_____

_____

_____

_____

_____

_____

_____

_____

_____

_____

3. Read over what you have written to discern if God is speaking to you. You may hear from him right away, or you may have to continue to practice this listening prayer as you continue to meditate on his Word.

Making It Personal

What a sweet time we have had together beholding the Lord in prayer. Let us close by beholding the Lord together as we lift up the name of Jesus.

Dear Lord,

Thank you for this sweet time we've had together beholding you. First, we pray that this work will be used to help many, including our own dear friends and family, so that they can behold you like never before.

Second, we thank you for sending your Son into this world to pay the price for our sin. We also thank you for sending your Holy Spirit to speak to us and to give us direction. Thank you for allowing us to use the name of your Son so that we can ask you for whatever we need so that our joy will be full.

Help us to remember that you are totally trustworthy and that one day, when we've trusted you through this life, we will join you in the life to come. In the meantime, we know your Holy Spirit is with us, guiding us and helping us to do your will, to tell others about the good news of Jesus, and to demonstrate your love.

Help us to overcome this world as we turn our anxious thoughts to you and keep our eyes on Jesus. Turn down the white noise of our thoughts and speak to us clearly as we practice listening for your voice. Our goal is to stay in continuing communion with you.

Like Peter, we choose to follow you. In Jesus's name, amen.

Discussion Questions

Introduction and Chapter 1:
Praying to Experience God's Presence

1. Jot down five prayer requests to bring before the Lord. During the prayer time, share the ones you'd like the group to help you pray over.

2. As a group, take turns or work together to explain why and how Jesus is the way to a relationship with God.

3. How does someone put "oil in their lamp" for the first time? Go back to the prayer about igniting your lamp for the first time and read it as a group.

4. Is there anyone in the group who's never prayed a prayer like this before? If you've pledged your faith in God through Jesus for the first time, congratulations! Take time to share the good news and celebrate with your group. If you've made this kind of pledge before, share the details of your first encounter with faith in God through Jesus.

5. What will help you walk through the storms of life? Explain how this concept helped Peter to walk on water and Linda to walk through her to-do list.

6. Read the "Beholding Jesus in Prayer" as a group. Next, discuss how you can apply this concept to a difficulty you are going through.

7. Have someone read the Scripture passage under "Listening Prayer," then each share what you wrote in the writing exercise segment.

8. Share prayer requests and pray for each person to behold Jesus in the situations shared.

Chapter 2: Experience God's Transforming Power

1. Share with the group the benefits you hope to find from developing a better prayer life. Also share what you think your main obstacles will be to fulfilling your goal and discuss how you might remedy those obstacles.

2. What are the prayer ABCs, and what do they stand for? Either as a group or individually, create an ABC prayer.

3. What is the prayer that Stormie Omartian recommends you pray? How do you think this prayer will make an impact on your personal life?

4. Explain what the veil of blindness is and how to remove it. Why do people still suffer from this blindness?

5. If God wants to transform your life, what would stop him from doing so? What can you do to experience God's transformation?

6. Why did Jesus say that Mary's choice was better than Martha's choice? What are some subtle things that will keep you from making Mary's choice? Make a plan to spend more time focusing on God and share it with the group.

7. What are the ways God wants to transform you? Which one of these attributes do you need to trust God for the most?

8. Have someone read the Scripture passage under "Listening Prayer," then each share what you wrote in the writing exercise segment.

9. Close in prayer for one another.

Chapter 3: Experience God's Blessings

1. When Linda had car trouble at the coffee shop, she felt blessed. Name some of her blessings, then compare that same story with Linda's negative telling of the story. What made the difference for Linda? How can you look for blessings in your own life?

2. Share the results of the exercise in which you listed blessings regarding a difficulty you are facing.

3. Read Matthew 5:3–12. Take turns listing and describing the blessings mentioned by Jesus. What do you think God is saying to you regarding this list?

4. Ask God to give you some ideas about how you individually and as a group can be a blessing to someone. List the ideas and pick one for a group project. Also name an idea that you think God may be calling you to do on your own. Give a report about how your project worked out the next time you meet.

5. What stood out to you concerning the story about Jesus blessing the children? What do you think God is saying to you through this story?

6. Read the "Beholding Jesus in Prayer" as a group.

7. Have someone read the Scripture passage under "Listening Prayer," then each share what you wrote in the writing exercise segment.

8. Close in prayer for one another.

Chapter 4: Experience God's Hope

1. Share how your idea, from last week, to bless someone worked out.

2. What are the three things you need to do when you feel your hope is waning? Can you describe how these three things have helped you in the past? Do you have any other suggestions to add?

3. Why does hopelessness sometimes make you feel disconnected from God? How does focusing on your sin, over focusing on God's grace, add to this problem? Do you think it's okay to keep on sinning? Why or why not?

4. Why is it important to choose hope? How does one do that? Read the prayer in this section together.

5. Have a volunteer read the poem in the "Take the Next Step" section. If you can relate to this poem with a personal example, share it. Discuss how this poem relates to Proverbs 16:9.

6. What stood out to you concerning the story about Jesus healing the lame man? What do you think God is saying to you through this story?

7. Read the "Beholding Jesus in Prayer" as a group.

8. Have someone read the Scripture passages under "Listening Prayer," then each share what you wrote in the writing exercise segment.

9. Close in prayer for one another.

Chapter 5: Experience Trusting in God

1. How did God turn what seemed like a lost prayer battle into the cornerstone of a miracle for Jess? Has God ever flipped what seemed like an unanswered prayer into a miracle in your life? If so, share it with the group.

2. What are the four things that are helpful to realize when things are not going your way?

3. Do you think what Linda says, "When we follow God, we are not lost," is true? Why or why not? Do you have an example?

4. How is God like a good father who wants to protect his children? How does the snake story illustrate what a good dad is like? What are the other qualities of a good father? Say this aloud: "Even if I did not have a good earthly dad, I have a good heavenly dad who loves and protects me." If you can think of an example of God's protection of you, please share it with the group.

5. Pray the prayer of peace as a group. Follow that by praying the "Beholding Jesus in Prayer" as a group.

6. What stood out to you concerning the story about the feeding of the multitude with five loaves and two fish? What do you think God is saying to you through this story?

7. Have someone read the Scripture passages under "Listening Prayer," then each share what you wrote in the writing exercise segment.

8. Close in prayer for one another.

Chapter 6: Experience Deliverance from Evil

1. What is the difference between rebuking the enemy and resisting him? What would be a good thing to tell the enemy if you want him out of your situation?

2. Discuss, one by one, the five best ways to resist the enemy.

3. Why does the enemy try to deceive believers? What can believers do about it? Does anyone in the group have a report to tell about what happened after breaking the enemy's lies in prayer? If so, please share it. As a group, pray the prayer to break the lies of the enemy.

4. Read Ephesians 6:13–18. What is the armor you can wear to ward off the enemy's attacks? Pray the armor prayer as a group prayer.

5. Why was Jesus able to cast out the enemy from the possessed boy when his disciples couldn't? Are there areas in your life that require much prayer? If you feel comfortable, share these requests with the group in your prayer time for one another.

6. Have someone read the Scripture passage under "Listening Prayer," then each share what you wrote in the writing exercise segment.

7. Close in prayer for one another.

Chapter 7: Experience God's Healing Power

1. What does Isaiah 53:5 say about healing?

2. Linda told about two prayer encounters for miracles. In the first example, a woman was healed of osteoarthritis, but in the other example, Linda's daughter was healed of some of her injuries but not all. Why do you think the results of the prayers varied? Do you agree with the statement that some people get physical healings on earth, while others get their longed-for healings in heaven? Why or why not?

3. Why is it important not to take our own lives?

4. Read Elmer Towns's quotation. Then discuss why God may not answer your every prayer.

5. Why should we pray in God's will?

6. Linda says it's always God's will to heal us spiritually and emotionally. Discuss Max Lucado's insight on how to seek wholeness. Pray as a group the prayer following Lucado's discussion of wholeness.

7. What stood out to you concerning the story of the healing of Peter's mother-in-law? What do you think God is saying to you through this story?

8. Have someone read the Scripture passage under "Listening Prayer," then each share what you wrote in the writing exercise segment.

9. Pray one of the healing prayers as a group. Then close in prayer for one another.

Chapter 8: Experience Praising God

1. Read Revelation 4:6–8. Explain how nature worships God and compare this to how you should worship God. What are the benefits you will get from worshiping God?

2. What were the elements inside the ark of the covenant? Explain all the ways your commitment to Christ symbolizes having the ark of the covenant in your very being.

3. Read (or sing) the Lord's Prayer together as an act of worship.

4. Describe how you would feel if Jesus Christ suddenly appeared in your group? What would you do or say to him? Now realize that he is with you right now. What will you do or say to him now?

5. What stood out to you concerning the story about Jesus healing the ten lepers? What do you think God is saying to you through this story?

6. Read the "Beholding Jesus in Prayer" as a group.

7. Have someone read the Scripture passage under "Listening Prayer," then each share what you wrote in the writing exercise segment.

8. Close in prayer for one another.

Chapter 9: Experience God's Love

1. Does God stop loving you when you goof up? What did Linda realize when she was sitting in her dark living room feeling like a failure? How does this apply to you?

2. Why does God clothe you in the righteousness of Christ? How does this compare to God clothing Adam and Eve with animal skins? Does this give you the license to sin more abundantly? Why or why not?

3. Explain how or why you are in God's heart.

4. What are three things that keep us from drawing near to God? Explain how you can overcome these obstacles.

5. Take turns reading the Scripture passages in the love exercise. Then as a group, pray the prayers together.

6. What is the key element of the story about Jesus washing Peter's feet and the story of Mary and Martha? Why is it important to let God serve you? Give some examples of how you can do that.

7. Have someone read the Scripture passage under "Listening Prayer," then each share what you wrote in the writing exercise segment.

8. Close in prayer for one another.

Chapter 10: Experience the Joy of the Lord

1. Discuss Lloyd John Ogilvie's claim that joy is our responsibility. How can this be true in the face of difficult circumstances? What did Linda do to regain her joy in the midst of her difficulties?

2. Discuss George Müller's strategy for joy. How did this help him accomplish more than an army of men in his day? How could you apply this strategy to your own life? Come up with several plans that could help you do so.

3. As a group, follow the instructions with the four meditation Scripture passages. Select volunteers to turn each Scripture passage into a prayer for your group.

4. Read Psalm 13, stopping to identify each section of the lament. Take time for each person in your group to create their own laments. Ask volunteers to share their laments with the group.

5. As a group, pray the prayer to break the spirit of trauma.

6. What is the key element of the story of the men walking to Emmaus? What do you think God is saying to you through this story? What part of the story impressed you the most?

7. Have someone read the Scripture passage under "Listening Prayer," then each share what you wrote in the writing exercise segment.

8. Close in prayer for one another.

Chapter 11: Experience the Peace of God

1. How did Linda's mother find peace despite her difficulties? How can her example encourage you?

2. How is God your ever-present help despite your (discuss the following one at a time) (1) problems, (2) worries, (3) fears.

3. As a group, pray together the prayer listed under the heading "Problems," then under the heading "Worries,"

then finally under the heading "Fears." What do you like most about each of these prayers?

4. Read the Billy Graham quotations and explain what they mean and discuss how to experience the meaning for yourself.

5. How did beholding Jesus change Saul's perspective? How can beholding Jesus change your perspective?

6. Read the "Beholding Jesus in Prayer" as a group. What does this prayer mean to you?

7. Have someone read the Scripture passages under "Listening Prayer," then each share what you wrote in the writing exercise segment.

8. Close in prayer for one another.

Chapter 12: Experience More of God

1. How did Linda finally hear God's voice when she lost her four-year-old son? Have there ever been times you heard God when you were in a crisis? Please share if you'd like.

2. What are the three steps that will help you hear from God? Also, how will reading Scripture help you hear God's voice?

3. What are the five ways that God might speak to you? Can you share with the group your favorite way or the way you are striving to hear God's voice?

4. What three things will keep you from hearing God's voice? Which, if any, do you struggle with the most?

5. Why is it so important to obey God? What kinds of things are in your safety net to ensure you are hearing God's voice and not something else?

6. What stood out to you concerning the story about Peter's call to follow Jesus? What do you think God is saying to you through this story?

7. Read the "Beholding Jesus in Prayer" as a group.

8. Have someone read the Scripture passages under "Listening Prayer," then each share what you wrote in the writing exercise segment.

9. Close in prayer for one another.

Notes

Chapter 1: Praying to Experience God's Presence

1. Mrs. Charles E. Cowman, *Streams in the Desert for Kids: 366 Devotionals to Bring Comfort* (Grand Rapids: Zonderkids, 2009), 273.

2. Will Davis, *Pray Big: The Power of Pinpoint Prayers* (Grand Rapids: Revell, 2007), 85.

Chapter 2: Experience God's Transforming Power

1. Rick Osborn, *Teaching Your Child How to Pray* (Chicago: Moody, 2000), 22.

2. Stanley G. Grenz, *Prayer, the Cry for the Kingdom* (Grand Rapids: Eerdmans, 2005), 124.

3. Stormie Omartian, *The Power of Praying: Help for a Woman's Journey through Life* (Eugene, OR: Harvest House, 2004), 106.

4. Matthew 13:33 TLB.

5. Linda Evans Shepherd, *When You Need a Miracle: How to Ask God for the Impossible* (Grand Rapids: Revell, 2012), 45–46.

6. Adrian Warnock, *Raised with Christ: How the Resurrection Changes Everything* (Wheaton: Crossway, 2010), 149.

Chapter 3: Experience God's Blessings

1. www.brainyquote.com/quotes/quotes/w/willienels381960.html.

2. Karla Dornacher, *Give Thanks* (Nashville: Thomas Nelson, 2001), 59.

3. http://thinkexist.com/quotes/with/keyword/blessings.

Chapter 4: Experience God's Hope

1. Rebekah Benimoff, *Faith Deployed: Daily Encouragement for Military Wives* (Chicago: Moody, 2009), 197.

2. Ray Pritchard, *Discovering God's Will for Your Life* (Wheaton: Crossway, 2004), 42.

3. Ibid., 46.

4. Lee Ezell, *Finding Hope When Life's Not Fair* (Grand Rapids: Revell, 2001), 193.

5. Max Lucado, *The Lucado Life Lessons Study Bible* (Nashville: Thomas Nelson, 1982), 738.

Chapter 6: Experience Deliverance from Evil

1. Charles Haddon Spurgeon, *Spurgeon on Prayer* (Alachua, FL: Bridge-Logos, 2009), 50.

2. R. C. Sproul, *1–2 Peter* (Wheaton: Crossway, 2011), 108.

3. Charles F. Stanley, *How to Reach Your Full Potential for God* (Nashville: Thomas Nelson, 2009), 217.

Chapter 7: Experience God's Healing Power

1. Elmer Towns, *How God Answers Prayer* (Shippensburg, PA: Destiny Image Publishers, 2009), chap. 32.

2. Beth Moore, *Breaking Free: Discover the Victory of Total Surrender* (Nashville: Broadman & Holman, 2007), 15.

3. Max Lucado, *Finding God Daily*, January 28, 2013, http://findinggoddaily.com/2013/01/27/max-lucado-finding-god-miracle-of-wholeness/

Chapter 8: Experience Praising God

1. *Christian Post*, September 24, 2011. http://m.christianpost.com/news/astronomy-fan-louie-giglio-shows-universe-is-playing-music-to-god-56433/.

2. *Adam Clarke's Commentary, Electronic Database* (Biblesoft, 1996).

3. Elmer Towns, *Praying the Lord's Prayer for Spiritual Breakthrough* (Ventura, CA: Regal, 1997), 18.

4. Rick Warren, *The Purpose Driven Life* (Grand Rapids: Zondervan, 2002), 64.

5. Based on a story by Eddie Ogan in Linda Evans Shepherd, *Heart-Stirring Stories of Love* (Nashville: Broadman & Holman, 2000), 7–10.

6. Based on a story by Thelma Wells in Linda Evans Shepherd and Eva Marie Everson, *Intimate Encounters with God* (Colorado Springs: Honor Books, 2003), 18–19.

7. Sarah Young, *Jesus Calling* (Nashville: Thomas Nelson, 2004), January 7.

Chapter 9: Experience God's Love

1. Linda Evans Shepherd, *When You Can't Find God: How to Ignite the Power of His Presence* (Grand Rapids: Revell, 2011), 149–50.

2. Henry Cloud and John Townsend, *God Will Make a Way* (Brentwood, TN: Integrity Publishers, 2002), 56.

3. Henry T. Blackaby and Claude V. King, *Experiencing God: Knowing and Doing the Will of God* (Nashville: Broadman & Holman, 2004), 16.

4. Max Lucado, *Just Like Jesus: Learning to Have a Heart Like Him* (Nashville: Thomas Nelson, 2003), 8.

Chapter 10: Experience the Joy of the Lord

1. Lloyd John Ogilvie, *Asking God Your Hardest Questions* (Colorado Springs: Waterbrook Press, 1986), 184.

2. http://en.wikipedia.org/wiki/George_M%C3%BCller.

3. Herman Lincoln, *The Life of Trust: The Lord's Dealings with George Müller* (New York: Sheldon and Company, 1873), 205.

4. Ibid.

5. Max Lucado, *Great Day Every Day: Navigating Life's Challenges with Promise and Purpose* (Nashville: Thomas Nelson, 2007), 50.

6. Psalm 22:16–18 NIV.

7. Isaiah 53:4–6 TLB.

8. Isaiah 53:7–9 TLB.

9. Isaiah 53:10 TLB.

Chapter 11: Experience the Peace of God

1. Sarah Young, *Jesus Calling,* February 5.
2. Billy Graham, *Unto the Hills: A Daily Devotional* (Nashville: Thomas Nelson, 2010), 6.
3. Ibid.

Chapter 12: Experience More of God

1. Ruth Graham, *Fear Not Tomorrow, God Is Already There* (New York: Howard Publishing, 2009), 119.
2. A. W. Tozer, *The Pursuit of God*, Google ebook, Mobile Reference, December 15, 2009.
3. Jack S. Deere, *Surprised by the Voice of God* (Grand Rapids: Zondervan, 1996), 232.
4. Henry T. Blackaby and Richard Blackaby, *Hearing God's Voice* (Nashville: Broadman & Holman, 2002), 214.

Linda Shepherd is the author of over thirty books, including *When You Can't Find God: How to Ignite the Power of His Presence*, *When You Don't Know What to Pray: How to Talk to God about Anything*, and *When You Need a Miracle: How to Ask God for the Impossible*.

An internationally recognized speaker, Linda has spoken in almost every state in the United States and in several countries around the world. You can learn more about her speaking ministry at www.LindaEvansShepherd.com.

Linda is the president of Right to the Heart Ministries. She is the CEO of AWSA (Advanced Writers and Speakers Association), which ministers to Christian women authors and speakers. This past year, Linda and the authors of AWSA created two new Right to the Heart ministries: a daily devotional (found at www.FindingGodDaily.com) and an outreach to the suicidal (found at www.ThinkingAboutSuicide.com).

To learn more about Linda's ministries, go to www. VisitLinda.com. Follow Linda on Twitter at @LindaShepherd or on Facebook at www.facebook.com/linda.e.shepherd.

Linda has been married to Paul for over thirty years and is the mother of two.

To find more information about this book, go to www. ExperienceGodBook.com or use the QR code below.

Connect with

Linda
Evans Shepherd

Blog www.gottopray.com

 Linda Evans Shepherd

LindaShepherd

Visit

www.sheppro.com

to book Linda to speak at
your next event.

WHEN YOU JUST DON'T KNOW WHAT TO SAY TO GOD . . .

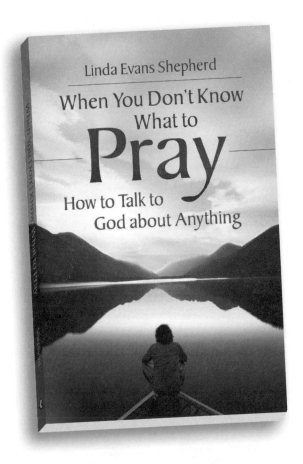

"A must-read for anyone who desires
a stronger prayer life."

—**Carole Lewis**, First Place National Director

"God makes the impossible possible every day."

—from the foreword by Don Piper, bestselling
author of *90 Minutes in Heaven*

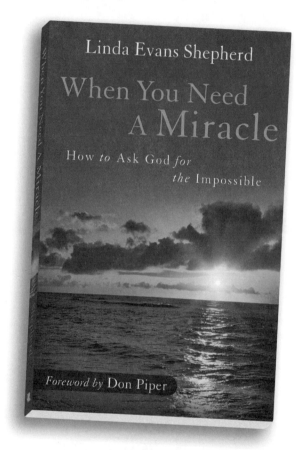

Through solid biblical teaching and dramatic real-life stories,
Shepherd walks with you on a journey of renewed hope and the
assurance that God still works miracles.